AFTER THE CRISIS

USING STORYBOOKS TO HELP CHILDREN COPE

BY CATHY GRACE AND ELIZABETH F. SHORES

ACKNOWLEDGMENTS

Many individuals and organizations contributed expertise and resources to the Rebuilding After Katrina Initiative. They include all of our colleagues at Mississippi State University, particularly Lynn Bell, Connie Clay, Denise Cox, Lynn Darling, Cathy Hollingshed, JoAnn Kelly, Annjo Lemons, Cheryl Mueller, and Pamela Myrick-Mottley of the MSU Early Childhood Institute and Louise E. Davis of the MSU Extension Service. These friends and advisors also include Gary Asmus, Amy Brandenstein, Carol Burnett, Todd Baptiste, Glenda Bean, Paula Bendel-Smith, Shannon Christian, Nadine Coleman, Jeanne-Aimee DeMarrais, Louisa Dixon, Sr. Donna Gunn, Gail Kelso, Paige Ellison-Smith, Emily Fenichel, Ouida Forsythe, Steven Gross, Sherry Guarisco, George Haddow, Moniquin Huggins, Laura Beth Hebbler, Hal Kaplan, Chad Landgraf, Rev. Bill McAlilly, Mary Ann McCabe, Gail McClure, Wendy McEarchern, Thomas Moore, Festus Simkins, Laurie Todd Smith, Julia Todd, Joy Osofsky, Linda Raft, Stephen Renfroe, Linda Smith, Billy Ray Stokes, Roy Winter, and the entire staff of the Center for Applied Research and Environmental Systems at the University of Missouri, particularly Erin W. Barbaro, Michael Barbaro, Michelle Flenner, Chad Landgraf, and Christopher L. Fulcher. Many other friends of young children also helped rebuild the early childhood sector. We learned from all of them.

DEDICATION

To the courageous individuals who lived through Hurricane Katrina with a determination to come back better than before; to the children and families who found comfort and strength in each other and have excelled in spite of trauma; and to those who came and stayed through the bad and the good so that the children of Katrina could laugh again.

and

To Charles Grace of Tupelo, Mississippi, and Buddy Johnson of Little Rock, Arkansas, for sticking with us through wind and high water.

GH13492
A Gryphon House Book

AFTER THE
CRISIS

USING STORYBOOKS
TO HELP CHILDREN COPE

Support Children After:

Earthquakes

Epidemics and Mass Casualty Incidents

Fires and Explosions

Floods

Hurricanes

Shelter Experiences

Tornadoes and Major Storms

Volcanic Eruptions

CATHY GRACE AND ELIZABETH F. SHORES

THE TEACHER'S COMPANION TO PREPARING FOR DISASTER

© 2010 Cathy Grace and Elizabeth F. Shores
Published by Gryphon House, Inc.
10770 Columbia Pike, Suite 201
Silver Spring, MD 20901
800.638.0928; 301.595.9500; 301.595.0051 (fax)

Visit us on the web at www.gryphonhouse.com

Cover Art: www.stockxpert.com

LIBRARY OF CONGRESS CATALOGING-IN-PUBLICATION INFORMATION:

Grace, Cathy.
 After the crisis : using storybooks to help children cope / by Cathy Grace and Elizabeth F. Shores.
     p. cm.
 Includes bibliographical references.
 ISBN 978-0-87659-129-1
 1. Disasters--Psychological aspects. 2. Psychic trauma in children--Treatment. 3. Bibliotherapy for children. 4. Art therapy for children. I. Shores, Elizabeth F. II. Title.
 BF723.D5G73 2010
 372.17'13--dc22

                          2009033703

TABLE OF CONTENTS

122933

LITERATURE-BASED OUTLETS FOR CREATIVE EXPRESSION

After a disaster affects a community, everyone, from the youngest infants to the most experienced teachers and mental health professionals, can suffer. Teachers are responsible for recognizing the signs that young children are suffering from continuing stress, for helping parents obtain appropriate assessment and, if necessary, treatment. Most early childhood teachers do not have the background or skills to provide therapy to children with traumatic stress disorder. However, in the classroom, teachers can help children understand and cope with frightening experiences. The literature-based activities in this book help teachers acknowledge the disaster and cope with their own feelings of fear and anxiety.

Within the familiar setting of the classroom, teachers can offer children many opportunities to discuss, reenact, and begin to understand their experiences and feelings—opportunities that can help children deal with stress (Greenspan & Wieder, 2006). With reading appropriate children's books during Circle Time or in small groups as the starting point, teachers can create many opportunities for creative expression through dramatic play using toy rescue vehicles, dolls, and other props, and through writing, art activities ,and extended projects (Devall & Cahill, 1995; Alat, 2002; Szente, Hoot, & Taylor, 2006). The goal is not to use the children's traumatic experiences as springboards for meeting curricular objectives in literacy, mathematics, or science, but to support children's deep emotional need to regain feelings of security.

When teachers give children creative outlets for remembering traumatic experiences and expressing fear, anger, and other emotions, they can expect children to describe or depict disturbing events and demonstrate strong feelings. Remembering and reenacting the disaster is appropriate and not necessarily a sign of social-emotional problems. Teachers are not the right professionals to interpret children's writing samples and artworks as evidence of mental health problems. If teachers share children's stories or artworks related to their disaster experiences with families or mental health professionals, they should make clear whether they elicited the storytelling and depiction. Otherwise, the children's work samples could be misinterpreted (Kindler, 1996).

The following books and activities are appropriate for teachers of two- to eight-year-olds to use during one-on-one, small-group, and whole-group reading times. The Discussion Starters and the open-ended activities for the writing and art centers in the classroom will allow and encourage children to talk and think about their experiences after a disaster.

Most of these books are available in at least 500 public libraries across the United States. A few titles are available in slightly fewer libraries but are outstanding resources for helping children cope.

With a little planning, you can obtain any of these books from your nearest public library by requesting an interlibrary loan. Your librarian can show you how to fill out an interlibrary loan request.

On the following pages, you will find library lists indicating whether each book can be used in year-round activities to promote social-emotional resilience or in activities to help children cope with various kinds of disasters. Many books will be useful after more than one kind of disaster.

The lists also indicate whether each book is useful for children ages 2–8 years, 3–8 years, or 5–8 years. Of course, these are generalizations and you may find the books to be appropriate for younger or older children. Many of the books on the lists would not be developmentally appropriate for most school-age children, but in the aftermath of traumatic experiences, some young children experience regression of developmental skills, so these books may be appropriate for them.

These books and activities also may be appropriate because they can encourage school-age children to take on the roles of a teacher or counselor, giving them ways to help each other.

IMPORTANT GUIDELINES TO REMEMBER WHEN WORKING WITH CHILDREN WHO HAVE EXPERIENCED A TRAUMA

Death is a difficult topic to discuss. Children who have lost family members or friends may want to talk about those who have died.

You can use books as springboards for general discussions of death in the disaster, but wait for individual children to bring up specific losses they have experienced. Follow the children's lead to determine when or where to talk about particular deaths.

Introduce each book by reading the title, author's name, and illustrator's name, pointing to each on the cover or initial pages.

Encourage the children to comment on the book as you read it aloud. Pause whenever the children want to discuss the story or illustrations.

If the book does not hold the children's interest, shorten the reading by discussing the events in the story without reading the book line by line. This is a good approach with books that have a useful topic but are a little advanced for the children.

After you introduce the book in this way, proceed with the suggestions for Discussion Starters as well as any other questions you want to add. Set up and explain materials and optional activities for the art and writing centers in the classroom. If several children are preoccupied with a disaster experience, or if a particular book engages their sustained interest, extend their exploration of the topic with "project" activities such as classroom exhibits.

As children's preoccupation with the disaster experience wanes, resume your planned curriculum.

REFERENCES

Alat, K. 2002. Traumatic events and children: How early childhood educators can help. *Childhood Education,* 79(1), 2–8.

Devall, E.L., & B.J. Cahill. 1995. Addressing children's life changes in the early childhood curriculum. *Early Childhood Education Journal,* 23(2), 57–62.

Greenspan, S.I., & S. Wieder. 2006. *Infant and early childhood mental health: A comprehensive, developmental approach to assessment and intervention.* Washington, DC: American Psychiatric Publishing, Inc.

Kindler, A.M. 1996. Myths, habits, research, and policy: The four pillars of early childhood art education. *Arts Education Policy Review,* 97(4), 24–30.

Szente, J., J. Hoot, & D. Taylor. 2006. Responding to the special needs of refugee children: Practical ideas for teachers. *Early Childhood Education Journal,* 34(1), 15–20.

LIBRARY LISTS

BOOKS THAT PROMOTE EMOTIONAL RESILIENCE

For 2- to 8-Year-Olds

Babies in the Bayou, by Jim Arnosky

Go Away, Big Green Monster! by Ed Emberley

The Grouchy Ladybug, by Eric Carle

"I'm Not Scared!" by Jonathan Allen

Mommy, Carry Me Please! by Jane Cabrera

Stina, by Lena Anderson

The Very Lonely Firefly, by Eric Carle

For 3- to 8-Year-Olds

Bear Feels Scared, by Karma Wilson and Jane Chapman (illustrator)

Dakota's Mom Goes to the Hospital, by Annie Thiel, Ph.D. and W. M. Edwards (illustrator)

Don't You Feel Well, Sam? by Amy Hest and Anita Jeram (illustrator)

Franklin and the Thunderstorm, by Paulette Bourgeois and Brenda Clark (illustrator)

Sam Is Never Scared, by Thierry Robberecht and Philippe Goossens (illustrator)

When the Big Dog Barks, by Munzee Curtis and Susan Avishai (illustrator)

For 5- to 8-Year-Olds

Terrible Storm, by Carol Otis Hurst and S.D. Schindler (illustrator)

BOOKS FOR HELPING CHILDREN COPE AFTER EARTHQUAKES

For 2- to 8-Year-Olds

"I'm Not Scared!" by Jonathan Allen

Rhinos Who Rescue, by Julie Mammano

The Very Lonely Firefly, by Eric Carle

For 3- to 8-Year-Olds

Earthquack! by Margie Palatini and Barry Moser (illustrator)

Even Firefighters Hug Their Moms, by Christine Kole MacLean and Mike Reed (illustrator)

The Little Fire Engine, by Lois Lenski

For 5- to 8-Year-Olds

Earthquake! On a Peaceful Spring Morning, Disaster Strikes San Francisco, by Shelley Tanaka and David Craig (illustrator)

Terrible Storm, by Carol Otis Hurst and S.D. Schindler (illustrator)

Volcanoes and Earthquakes, by Susanna Van Rose

BOOKS FOR HELPING CHILDREN COPE AFTER EPIDEMICS AND MASS CASUALTY INCIDENTS

For 2- to 8-Year-Olds

Babies in the Bayou, by Jim Arnosky

"I'm Not Scared!" by Jonathan Allen

Mommy, Carry Me Please! by Jane Cabrera

Who's Sick Today? by Lynne Cherry

For 3- to 8-Year-Olds

Dakota's Mom Goes to the Hospital, by Annie Thiel, Ph.D. and W. M. Edwards (illustrator)

Don't You Feel Well, Sam? by Amy Hest and Anita Jeram (illustrator)

The Emergency Room, by Anne F. Rockwell and Harlow Rockwell

I Remember Miss Perry, by Pat Brisson and Stephane Jorisch (illustrator)

Miss Bindergarten Stays Home from Kindergarten, by Joseph Slate and Ashley Wolff (illustrator)

Sam Is Scared, by Thierry Robberecht and Philippe Goossens (illustrator)

William and the Good Old Days, by Eloise Greenfield and Jan Spivey Gilchrist (illustrator)

For 5- to 8-Year-Olds

Tough Topics: Death, by Patricia Murphy

BOOKS FOR HELPING CHILDREN COPE AFTER FIRES AND EXPLOSIONS

For 2- to 8-Year-Olds

Rhinos Who Rescue, by Julie Mammano

For 3- to 8-Year-Olds

Even Firefighters Hug Their Moms, by Christine Kole MacLean and Mike Reed (illustrator)

The Little Fire Engine, by Lois Lenski

BOOKS FOR HELPING CHILDREN COPE AFTER FLOODS

For 2- to 8-Year-Olds

Babies in the Bayou, by Jim Arnosky

Dot the Fire Dog, by Lisa Desimini

"I'm Not Scared!" by Jonathan Allen

In the Middle of the Puddle, by Mike Thaler and Bruce Degen (illustrator)

Mommy, Carry Me Please! by Jane Cabrera

Stina, by Lena Anderson

For 3- to 8-Year-Olds

A Shelter in Our Car, by Monica Gunning and Elaine Pedlar (illustrator)

Cock-a-doodle-hooooooo! by Mick Manning and Brita Granstrom (illustrator)

Even Firefighters Hug Their Moms, by Christine Kole MacLean and Mike Reed (illustrator)

Franklin and the Thunderstorm, by Paulette Bourgeois and Brenda Clark (illustrator)

It's Mine! by Leo Lionni

Just You and Me, by Sam McBratney and Ivan Bates (illustrator)

Sam Is Never Scared, by Thierry Robberecht and Philippe Goossens (illustrator)

Ten Little Rubber Ducks, by Eric Carle

We Hate Rain! by James Stevenson

When the Big Dog Barks, by Munzee Curtis and Susan Avishai (illustrator)

For 5- to 8-Year-Olds

River Friendly, River Wild, by Jane Kurtz and Neil Brennan (illustrator)

Terrible Storm, by Carol Otis Hurst and S.D. Schindler (illustrator)

BOOKS FOR HELPING CHILDREN COPE AFTER HURRICANES

For 2- to 8-Year-Olds

Babies in the Bayou, by Jim Arnosky

Chicky Chicky Chook Chook, by Cathy MacLennan

Dot the Fire Dog, by Lisa Desimini

"I'm Not Scared!" by Jonathan Allen

Mommy, Carry Me Please! by Jane Cabrera

Stina, by Lena Anderson

For 3- to 8-Year-Olds

Cock-a-doodle-hooooooo! by Mick Manning and Brita Granstrom (illustrator)

Even Firefighters Hug Their Moms, by Christine Kole MacLean and Mike Reed (illustrator)

Franklin and the Thunderstorm, by Paulette Bourgeois and Brenda Clark (illustrator)

It's Mine! by Leo Lionni

Just You and Me, by Sam McBratney and Ivan Bates (illustrator)

A Shelter in Our Car, by Monica Gunning and Elaine Pedlar (illustrator)

Ten Little Rubber Ducks, by Eric Carle

When the Big Dog Barks, by Munzee Curtis and Susan Avishai (illustrator)

For 5- to 8-Year-Olds

Terrible Storm, by Carol Otis Hurst and S.D. Schindler (illustrator)

BOOKS FOR HELPING CHILDREN COPE AFTER SHELTER EXPERIENCES

For 2- to 8-Year-Olds

Footprints in the Snow, by Cynthia Benjamin and Jacqueline Rogers (illustrator)

A House of Leaves, by Soya Kiyoshi and A. Hayashi (illustrator)

Stina, by Lena Anderson

For 3- to 8-Year-Olds

Cock-a-doodle-hooooooo! by Mick Manning and Brita Granstrom (illustrator)

Flashlight, by Betsy James and Stacey Schuett (illustrator)

Fly Away Home, by Eve Bunting and Ronald Himler (illustrator)

Franklin and the Thunderstorm, by Paulette Bourgeois and Brenda Clark (illustrator)

It's Mine! by Leo Lionni

Just You and Me, by Sam McBratney and Ivan Bates (illustrator)

The Owl and the Woodpecker, by Brian Wildsmith

A Shelter in Our Car, by Monica Gunning and Elaine Pedlar (illustrator)

For 5- to 8-Year-Olds

Earthquake! On a Peaceful Spring Morning, Disaster Strikes San Francisco, by Shelley Tanaka and David Craig (illustrator)

River Friendly, River Wild, by Jane Kurtz and Neil Brennan (illustrator)

Terrible Storm, by Carol Otis Hurst and S.D. Schindler (illustrator)

Tornado, by Betsy Byars and Doron Ben-Ami (illustrator)

Volcanoes, by Seymour Simon

BOOKS FOR HELPING CHILDREN COPE AFTER TORNADOES AND MAJOR STORMS

For 2- to 8-Year-Olds

Babies in the Bayou, by Jim Arnosky

Chicky Chicky Chook Chook, by Cathy MacLennan

Dot the Fire Dog, by Lisa Desimini

Footprints in the Snow, by Cynthia Benjamin and Jacqueline Rogers (illustrator)

A House of Leaves, by Soya Kiyoshi and A. Hayashi (illustrator)

If Frogs Made the Weather, by Marion Dane Bauer and Dorothy Donohue (illustrator)

"I'm Not Scared!" by Jonathan Allen

Mommy, Carry Me Please! by Jane Cabrera

Rain, by Peter Spier

The Snowy Day, by Ezra Jack Keats

Stina, by Lena Anderson

That Sky, That Rain, by Carolyn Otto and Megan Lloyd (illustrator)

The Very Lonely Firefly, by Eric Carle

For 3- to 8-Year-Olds

Bear Feels Scared, by Karma Wilson and Jane Chapman (illustrator)

Clifford and the Big Storm, by Norman Bridwell

Cock-a-doodle-hooooooo! by Mick Manning and Brita Granstrom (illustrator)

Even Firefighters Hug Their Moms, by Christine Kole MacLean and Mike Reed (illustrator)

Flashlight, by Betsy James and Stacey Schuett (illustrator)

It's Mine! by Leo Lionni

Just You and Me, by Sam McBratney and Ivan Bates (illustrator)

The Owl and the Woodpecker, by Brian Wildsmith

Policeman Lou and Policewoman Sue, by Lisa Desimini

Sam Is Never Scared, by Thierry Robberecht and Philippe Goossens (illustrator)

A Shelter in Our Car, by Monica Gunning and Elaine Pedlar (illustrator)

Storm in the Night, by Mary Stolz and Pat Cummings (illustrator)

Take Time to Relax! by Nancy Carlson

Ten Little Rubber Ducks, by Eric Carle

We Hate Rain! by James Stevenson

When the Big Dog Barks, by Munzee Curtis and Susan Avishai (illustrator)

For 5- to 8-Year-Olds

Terrible Storm, by Carol Otis Hurst and S.D. Schindler (illustrator)

Tornado, by Betsy Byars and Doron Ben-Ami (illustrator)

The Tornado Watches, by Patrick Jennings and Anna Alter (illustrator)

BOOKS FOR HELPING CHILDREN COPE AFTER VOLCANIC ERUPTIONS

For 3- to 8-Year-Olds

The Little Fire Engine, by Lois Lenski

For 5- to 8-Year-Olds

Volcanoes, by Seymour Simon

Volcanoes and Earthquakes, by Susanna Van Rose

BABIES IN THE BAYOU

BY JIM ARNOSKY

The mothers of all the baby animals in the bayou keep a watchful eye on their children to feed them and protect them.

APPROPRIATE FOR:

Earthquakes

▶ **Emotional Resilience**

▶ **Epidemics and Mass Casualty Incidents**

Fires and Explosions

▶ **Floods**

▶ **Hurricanes**

Shelter Experiences

▶ **Tornadoes and Major Storms**

Volcanic Eruptions

DISCUSSION STARTERS

Use the following prompts to encourage the children to talk about their experiences, either in the context of the book or in the context of a traumatic experience.

For 2- to 8-Year-Olds

- How do mothers take care of their babies?
- Who protects you? How does that person protect you?
- What about your father or grandmother or maybe an aunt? How do they protect you?

For 5- to 8-Year-Olds

- How does the mother alligator protect her babies?
- The mother raccoon? The mother duck?
- How do grown-ups protect you?

After a Rescue or Traumatic Experience | Use the following prompts to invite children to talk about their experiences.
- How did grown-ups protect you in our storm?
- If you were a grown-up, how would you protect your baby?

ART CENTER OPTIONS

For 3- to 8-Year-Olds

- Cut out magazine pictures of people who remind you of someone who protected or rescued you.
- Draw a picture of one of the animals in *Babies in the Bayou.*
- Draw a picture of a grown-up who protects you.
- Draw a picture of what happened one time when a grown-up protected you.

WRITING CENTER OPTIONS

For 3- to 8-Year-Olds

- Dictate or write a sentence or story to go with your picture.

BEAR FEELS SCARED

BY KARMA WILSON AND JANE CHAPMAN (ILLUSTRATOR)

When a big storm comes up in the forest, Bear cannot find his way home. His brave friend makes all the difference.

APPROPRIATE FOR:

Earthquakes
▶ **Emotional Resilience**
Epidemics and Mass Casualty Incidents
Fires and Explosions
Floods
Hurricanes
Shelter Experiences
▶ **Tornadoes and Major Storms**
Volcanic Eruptions

DISCUSSION STARTERS

Use the following prompts to encourage the children to talk about their experiences, either in the context of the book or in the context of a traumatic experience.

For 3- to 8-Year-Olds

- What happened to Bear?
- How did Bear feel?
- Do you ever feel scared? How does "scared" feel?
- Did you feel scared in our big storm? How did you get "un-scared"?

For 5- to 8-Year-Olds

- Look at Jane Chapman's illustrations:
  - She painted long strokes of color on dark backgrounds.
  - Could you use pastels or chalks or crayons to make marks like her strokes?

> **After a Rescue Experience |** Use the following prompts to invite children to talk about their experiences.
> - Who rescued Bear? How was he rescued?
> - Did someone rescue you and your family in our big storm?
> - Did you stop feeling scared when you were rescued?

ART CENTER OPTIONS

For 3- to 8-Year-Olds

- Draw a picture of one of the animals in the story.
- Draw a picture of what you did in our big storm.

For 5- to 8-Year-Olds

- Draw a picture of something you would do to rescue someone in a storm.
- Experiment with Jane Chapman's technique:
  - Use pastels, chalks, or crayons to make marks on paper.
  - Use brushes to stroke paint on the paper.

Extended Project

- Combine multiple artworks, inspired by Jane Chapman's techniques, and stories about our storm in a class exhibit.

WRITING CENTER OPTIONS

For 3- to 8-Year-Olds

- Dictate or write a sentence or story to go with your picture.
- Dictate or write a sentence or story about how you made your picture.

Extended Project

- Dictate or write a label or text panel for a classroom exhibit about our storm.

CHICKY CHICKY CHOOK CHOOK

BY CATHY MACLENNAN

The little chicks are playing and napping in the sun when—oops—rain! How will they ever get dry?

APPROPRIATE FOR:
Earthquakes
Emotional Resilience
Epidemics and Mass Casualty
   Incidents
Fires and Explosions
Floods
▶ **Hurricanes**
Shelter Experiences
▶ **Tornadoes and Major
   Storms**
Volcanic Eruptions

DISCUSSION STARTERS
Use the following prompts to encourage the children to talk about their experiences, either in the context of the book or in the context of a traumatic experience.

For 2- to 8-Year-Olds
- What happened in the story when the rain came down?
- What happened in our storm (or hurricane)?
- Did you hear thunder?
- Did you see lightning?
- Did you get wet?
- Did anything happen to your house?
- What happened at the end of the story?
- Did the sun come out where we live?

For 5- to 8-Year-Olds
- Look at Cathy MacLennan's pictures:
   - She used brown paper.
   - She used a sponge to dab on yellow and white paint.
   - She used wide brushes to paint blue, black, green, white and orange.
   - She used a narrow brush to paint black and red edges and lines.

ART CENTER OPTIONS

For 5- to 8-Year-Olds
- Make a picture of what happened to the chicks.
- Make a picture of what happened at your house during our storm (or hurricane).

For 5- to 8-Year-Olds
- Experiment with Cathy MacLennan's techniques:
   - Use brown paper
   - Use sponges
   - Use wide brushes
   - Use narrow brushes
- Make a picture using one or more of Cathy MacLennan's techniques.

WRITING CENTER OPTIONS

For 3- to 8-Year-Olds
- Dictate or write a sentence or story about the chicks in *Chicky Chicky Chook Chook*.
- Dictate or write a sentence or story about our storm (or hurricane).
- Dictate or write a sentence or story about how you feel now that our storm (or hurricane) is over.

For 5- to 8-Year-Olds
- Dictate or write a sentence or story about how you made your picture.

CLIFFORD AND THE BIG STORM

BY NORMAN BRIDWELL

A hurricane blows ashore while Emily is visiting her grandmother. Fortunately, Clifford the dog is there, and he knows exactly what to do.

APPROPRIATE FOR:

Earthquakes
Emotional Resilience
Epidemics and Mass Casualty
    Incidents
Fires and Explosions
Floods
Hurricanes
▶ **Shelter Experiences**
▶ **Tornadoes and Major
    Storms**
Volcanic Eruptions

DISCUSSION STARTERS

Use the following prompts to encourage the children to talk about their experiences, either in the context of the book or in the context of a traumatic experience.

For 3- to 8-Year-Olds

■ The wind blew people and houses through the air. Did we have a wind that blew things through the air?

After a Shelter Experience | Use the following prompts to invite children to talk about their shelter experiences.

■ People in this story had to evacuate their homes. Did you have to evacuate your home when we had our big storm?

■ The people in this storm went to a shelter at a high school. Did you go to a shelter?

■ Where was your shelter?

■ Did you have a cot to sleep on? Did you sleep on the floor?

■ If you had a pet, what happened to your pet in our big storm?

ART CENTER OPTIONS

For 3- to 8-Year-Olds

■ Draw a picture of your pet and what happened in our big storm.

■ Draw a picture of something you would take with you if you had to evacuate your home.

After a Shelter Experience

■ Draw a picture of where you went when you evacuated during our big storm.

WRITING CENTER OPTIONS

For 3- to 8-Year-Olds

■ Dictate or write a sentence or story about your picture.

COCK-A-DOODLE-HOOOOOOO!

BY MICK MANNING AND
BRITA GRANSTROM
(ILLUSTRATOR)

A little owl seeks shelter in a henhouse during a nighttime storm. At first, the hens object to his intrusion but in the end everyone appreciates each other.

Note: At the time we prepared these activities, this 2007 release was available in only 107 public libraries nationwide, less than our standard of 500. However, we include it here because the story and illustrations can help young children think about their experiences in several kinds of disasters and in shelters and because we expect the book to become more widely available.

APPROPRIATE FOR:

Earthquakes
Emotional Resilience
Epidemics and Mass Casualty
    Incidents
Fires and Explosions
▶ **Floods**
▶ **Hurricanes**
▶ **Shelter Experiences**
▶ **Tornadoes and Major**
    Storms
Volcanic Eruptions

DISCUSSION STARTERS

Use the following prompts to encourage the children to talk about their experiences, either in the context of the book or in the context of a traumatic experience.

For 3- to 8-Year-Olds

- Why did Owl stay in the henhouse?
- Did you have to stay with strangers when we had our storm (or other disaster)? If so, how did that make you feel?
- Did the hens seem nice at first? Why?
- Did the hens become nicer to Owl? What did they do?
- How did Owl help the hens?

After a Shelter Experience | Use the following prompts to invite children to talk about their shelter experiences.

- Did you have to stay somewhere else when we had our storm (or other disaster)?
- Did the people at your shelter seem nice? Why do you feel that way?
- Did people at your shelter become nicer to you? What did they do?
- Did you have a chance to help anyone at your shelter? What did you do? How did that make you feel?

ART CENTER OPTIONS

For 3- to 8-Year-Olds

- Draw a picture about what you did in our storm (or other disaster).
- Draw a picture about something you did when you stayed in a shelter.

WRITING CENTER OPTIONS

For 3- to 8-Year-Olds

- Dictate or write a sentence or story to go with your picture.
- Dictate or write a letter to someone you met at your shelter.
- Dictate or write a list of nice things that happened to you while you were at a shelter.

DAKOTA'S MOM GOES TO THE HOSPITAL

BY ANNIE THIEL, PH. D., AND W. M. EDWARDS (ILLUSTRATOR)

Everything is very different at home when Mom is in the hospital. Dad takes good care of her, but Dakota worries. When will Mom come home?

APPROPRIATE FOR:

Earthquakes
▶ **Emotional Resilience**
▶ **Epidemics and Mass Casualty Incidents**
Fires and Explosions
Floods
Hurricanes
Shelter Experiences
Tornadoes and Major Storms
Volcanic Eruptions

DISCUSSION STARTERS

Use the following prompts to encourage the children to talk about their experiences, either in the context of the book or in the context of a traumatic experience.

For 3- to 8-Year-Olds

- Where did Dakota's mom go?
- What happened after that?
- What did Dakota's dad do?

For 5- to 8-Year-Olds

- Let's look at the author's "Things You Can Do" list.
- Did you do any of these things when someone you know was in the hospital? Which ones?

> **After a Family Member's Serious Illness** | Use the following prompts to invite children to talk about their experiences.
> - Do you know anyone who had to go to a hospital?
> - How did that make you feel?
> - Did you ever feel mad like Dakota? When?
> - What about sad? Confused? Scared?
> - What about when a sick person came home? Was it hard to be cheerful? Why?

ART CENTER OPTIONS

For 3- to 8-Year-Olds

- Draw a picture of a time when someone went to the hospital.
- Draw a picture for someone who is sick or in the hospital.

For 5- to 8-Year-Olds

- Draw a picture of something you would do if you worked in a hospital.

WRITING CENTER OPTIONS

For 3- to 8-Year-Olds

- Dictate or write a sentence or story to go with your picture.
- Dictate or write a letter to the sick person to go with your picture.

DON'T YOU FEEL WELL, SAM?

BY AMY HEST AND ANITA JERAM (ILLUSTRATOR)

Sam does not feel well, and he does not want to take his medicine. Mother finds a cozy way to help him.

APPROPRIATE FOR:
Earthquakes
▶ **Emotional Resilience**
▶ **Epidemics and Mass Casualty Incidents**
Fires and Explosions
Floods
Hurricanes
Shelter Experiences
Tornadoes and Major Storms
Volcanic Eruptions

DISCUSSION STARTERS

Use the following prompts to encourage the children to talk about their experiences, either in the context of the book or in the context of a traumatic experience.

For 3- to 8-Year-Olds
- What was Sam afraid of?
- What was outside that Sam's mother was watching for?
- Did Sam's mother take care of him when he was sick? How do you know?
- Do we need someone to take care of us when we are sick? What should they do?

ART CENTER OPTIONS

For 3- to 8-Year-Olds
- Draw a picture of a time when you were sick and someone took care of you.

WRITING CENTER OPTIONS

For 3- to 8-Year-Olds
- Dictate or write a sentence or story to go with your picture.
- Dictate or write a letter to someone who took care of you when you were sick:

  Dear _____: I liked it when you _____.

DOT THE FIRE DOG

BY LISA DESIMINI

We see a day in the life of Dot, the Dalmatian who lives at the firehouse, and the brave firefighters who do their jobs every day.

APPROPRIATE FOR:

Earthquakes
Emotional Resilience
Epidemics and Mass Casualty Incidents
Fires and Explosions
▶ **Floods**
▶ **Hurricanes**
Shelter Experiences
▶ **Tornadoes and Major Storms**
Volcanic Eruptions

DISCUSSION STARTERS

Use the following prompts to encourage the children to talk about their experiences, either in the context of the book or in the context of a traumatic experience.

For 2- to 8-Year-Olds

- Who does Dot the Fire Dog help?
- Who do the firefighters help?
- How do the firefighters help the man?
- How would firefighters rescue you in a fire?
- How could firefighters help people in a hurricane?
- Look at how Lisa Desimini painted the pictures:
  - ❏ She used a brush to dab black paint over white to make Dot's spots.

After a Rescue Experience | Use the following prompts to invite children to talk about their rescue experiences.
- Did firefighters rescue you when we had our storm?
- Did someone else rescue you or someone in your family?
- What happened when they rescued you or someone in your family?

ART CENTER OPTIONS

For 3- to 8-Year-Olds

- Draw a picture of a firefighter.
- Draw a picture of a time when someone rescued you or someone in your family.

For 5- to 8-Year-Olds

- Experiment with Lisa Desimini's technique:
  - ❏ Use a brush to dab black paint over white to make spots.

WRITING CENTER OPTIONS

For 3- to 8-Year-Olds

- Dictate or write a sentence or story about a firefighter who rescues someone.
- Dictate or write a sentence or story about a time when someone rescued you or someone in your family.

For 5- to 8-Year-Olds

- Dictate or write a sentence or story about how you made your picture.

EARTHQUACK!

**BY MARGIE PALATINI AND
BARRY MOSER
(ILLUSTRATOR)**

An earthquake story, which features some nervous barnyard animals and a wily weasel. It may remind you of Henny-Penny and "The sky is falling!"

APPROPRIATE FOR:

▶ **Earthquakes**
Emotional Resilience
Epidemics and Mass Casualty
  Incidents
Fires and Explosions
Floods
Hurricanes
Shelter Experiences
Tornadoes and Major Storms
Volcanic Eruptions

DISCUSSION STARTERS

Use the following prompts to encourage the children to talk about their experiences, either in the context of the book or in the context of a traumatic experience.

For 3- to 8-Year-Olds

- Was our earthquake imaginary like Chucky Ducky's earthquake? Why do you think so?
- Did you feel the earth rumble in our earthquake? Can you tell us how it made your insides feel?
- Did you want to warn your friends?
- Did you see the earthquake happen? What did you see?

ART CENTER OPTIONS

For 3- to 8-Year-Olds

- Draw a picture of what you were doing in our earthquake.
- Use playdough to make buildings or houses that were damaged in an earthquake and work with a partner to fix them.

WRITING CENTER OPTIONS

For 3- to 8-Year-Olds

- Dictate or write a sentence or story to go with your picture.
- Dictate or write a letter to someone who took care of you during our earthquake.
- Choose a name for our earthquake (the way hurricanes have names) and let other children choose names, too; vote on the best name for our earthquake.

EARTHQUAKE!
ON A PEACEFUL SPRING MORNING, DISASTER STRIKES SAN FRANCISCO

BY SHELLEY TANAKA AND DAVID CRAIG (ILLUSTRATOR)

The story of the famous San Francisco earthquake and fire of 1906, told in the voices of four young survivors. Archival photographs and maps enhance the drama.

Note: At the time we prepared these activities, this book was available in only 459 public libraries nationwide, less than our standard of 500. However, we include it here because the illustrations can help young children comprehend earthquakes and because it can prompt children's discussions of shelter experiences.

APPROPRIATE FOR:
▶ **Earthquakes**
　Emotional Resilience
　Epidemics and Mass Casualty
　　Incidents
　Fires and Explosions
　Floods
　Hurricanes
▶ **Shelter Experiences**
　Tornadoes and Major Storms
　Volcanic Eruptions

DISCUSSION STARTERS

Use the following prompts to encourage the children to talk about their experiences, either in the context of the book or as a springboard to more personal discussions.

For 5- to 8-Year-Olds
- Is this a fact book or fiction? Why?
- Do the pictures look like what happened in our earthquake? Why?
- What possessions did you and your family lose in our earthquake?

After a Shelter Experience | Use the following prompts to invite children to talk about their shelter experiences.
- Look at the pictures of the tent cities in San Francisco on pages 22, 27, and 38 of *Earthquake!*
- Did you and your family stay in a tent city or other kind of shelter after our earthquake?

ART CENTER OPTIONS

For 5- to 8-Year-Olds
- Look at the photos for ideas about what happens in earthquakes.
- Draw a picture of something that happened in our earthquake.
- Draw a picture of something you and your family lost in our earthquake.

After a Shelter Experience | **For 5- to 8-Year-Olds**
- Draw a picture of the shelter where your family stayed after our earthquake.
- Draw a picture of a tent city.

WRITING CENTER OPTIONS

For 5- to 8-Year-Olds
- Dictate or write a sentence or story to go with your picture.
- Dictate or write a list of possessions you and your family lost in our earthquake.

After a Shelter Experience
- Dictate or write a sentence or story about the shelter where your family stayed after our earthquake.

Extended Project
- Combine lists of lost possessions into a catalog of items that children and their families need help to replace.

THE EMERGENCY ROOM

BY ANNE F. ROCKWELL
AND HARLOW ROCKWELL

By following what happens when a patient comes in with a sprained ankle, we get an understanding of the procedures and equipment in the emergency room.

APPROPRIATE FOR:

Earthquakes
Emotional Resilience
▶ **Epidemics and Mass Casualty Incidents**
Fires and Explosions
Floods
Hurricanes
Shelter Experiences
Tornadoes and Major Storms
Volcanic Eruptions

DISCUSSION STARTERS

Use the following prompts to encourage the children to talk about their experiences, either in the context of the book or in the context of a traumatic experience.

For 3- to 8-Year-Olds

- Do you know anyone who has gone to a hospital? Who went and why did they have to go?
- Have you ever visited someone at a hospital? What was that like?
- Have you gone to a hospital because you were sick? What do you remember about that?
- Did you see any of the things in this book? What things did you see?
- Did the sick person you know get to go home right away?

ART CENTER OPTIONS

For 3- to 8-Year-Olds

- Draw a picture of someone who is sick.
- Draw a picture of what you think a hospital emergency room looks like.
- Draw a picture of someone at a hospital who takes care of sick people.
- With a partner, use a shoebox, construction paper, and other materials to make a hospital emergency room.

WRITING CENTER OPTIONS

For 3- to 8-Year-Olds

- Dictate or write a sentence or story to go with your picture or shoebox emergency room.
- Dictate or write signs for a hospital emergency room in the dramatic play center.

EVEN FIREFIGHTERS HUG THEIR MOMS

BY CHRISTINE KOLE MACLEAN AND MIKE REED (ILLUSTRATOR)

An imaginative little boy plays at being a firefighter, a doctor, a police officer, and more. This is an excellent springboard to conversation and to dramatic play.

APPROPRIATE FOR:

▶ **Earthquakes**
   Emotional Resilience
   Epidemics and Mass Casualty
      Incidents
▶ **Fires and Explosions**
▶ **Floods**
▶ **Hurricanes**
▶ **Tornadoes and Major
      Storms**
   Shelter Experiences
   Volcanic Eruptions

DISCUSSION STARTERS

Use the following prompts to encourage the children to talk about their experiences, either in the context of the book or in the context of a traumatic experience.

For 3- to 8-Year-Olds
- Is the boy in the story really a firefighter? Why do you think so?
- Do you like to pretend that you are a firefighter or someone else?
- Can you pretend to be a rescuer when you play in our Dramatic Play Center?

For 5- to 8-Year-Olds
- Does the boy look like the firefighters who helped people in our big storm (or other disaster)?
- What do firefighters need to do their jobs?

> **After a Rescue Experience** | Use the following prompt to invite children to talk about their shelter experiences.
> - Does the boy look like the rescuers who rescued you or your family in our big storm (or other disaster)? Why do you think so?

ART CENTER OPTIONS

For 3- to 8-Year-Olds
- Draw a picture of a time when you played in our Dramatic Play Center.
- Draw a picture of a firefighter or other rescuer.

> **After a Rescue Experience**
> - Draw a picture of how you and your family were rescued during our big storm (or other disaster).

WRITING CENTER OPTIONS

For 3- to 8-Year-Olds
- Dictate or write a sentence or story about how you made your picture.
- Dictate or write a sentence or story about rescuers in our big storm (or other disaster).

For 5- to 8-Year-Olds
- Dictate or write a list of things that firefighters need to rescue people.

> **After a Rescue Experience**
> - Dictate or write a thank-you letter to the rescuers who helped you and your family.

FLASHLIGHT

BY BETSY JAMES AND STACEY SCHUETT (ILLUSTRATOR)

Marie is nervous spending the night on the fold-out couch in her grandfather's living room. Her understanding Grandpa gives her a flashlight so she won't feel alone in the dark.

APPROPRIATE FOR:

Earthquakes

Emotional Resilience

Epidemics and Mass Casualty
   Incidents

Fires and Explosions

Floods

Hurricanes

▶ **Shelter Experiences**

▶ **Tornadoes and Major
   Storms**

Volcanic Eruptions

DISCUSSION STARTERS

Use the following prompts to encourage the children to talk about their experiences, either in the context of the book or in the context of a traumatic experience.

For 3- to 8-Year-Olds

- Did the lights go off where you were when we had our big storm? How did you see in the dark?
- Did you have a flashlight when the lights went off?
- Did a grown-up make you feel safe when the lights went off?

For 5- to 8-Year-Olds

- Look at Stacey Schuett's pictures:
  - She used black paper to make the house look dark.
  - She used yellow and pink chalk to make light shining in the dark.

After a Shelter Experience | Use the following prompts to invite children to talk about their shelter experiences.

- Did you go somewhere else to stay during our big storm?
- Where did you stay? What did you like best about staying there?
- Were your grandparents with you?
- Were there strangers where you stayed?
- Did you feel nervous like the girl in the book? What does "nervous" feel like?

ART CENTER OPTIONS

For 3- to 8-Year-Olds

- Draw a picture of your grandfather or someone who makes you feel safe.
- Draw a picture of a time when you stayed at someone else's house.

For 5- to 8-Year-Olds

- Use black paper and bright chalk to draw pictures of light in the dark.

After a Shelter Experience

- Draw a picture of the shelter where you stayed.

WRITING CENTER OPTIONS

For 3- to 8-Year-Olds

- Dictate or write a list of things someone could do to make you feel safe.
- Dictate or write a sentence or story to go with your picture.

FLY AWAY HOME

BY EVE BUNTING AND RONALD HIMLER (ILLUSTRATOR)

After his mother's death, apparently because of the loss of family income, pre-kindergartener Andrew and his father begin to live at an airport. Seeing a lost bird escape the airport through an open door, Andrew remains hopeful that he and his father will find a new home.

APPROPRIATE FOR:

Earthquakes

Emotional Resilience

Epidemics and Mass Casualty Incidents

Fires and Explosions

Floods

Hurricanes

▶ **Shelter Experiences**

Tornadoes and Major Storms

Volcanic Eruptions

DISCUSSION STARTERS

Use the following prompts to encourage the children to talk about their experiences, either in the context of the book or in the context of a traumatic experience.

For 5- to 8-Year-Olds

- Have you ever been to an airport?
- What do you think an airport would be like as a shelter if you were homeless?
- How did Andrew feel about his father? How did Andrew feel about the bird?
- Do you ever feel that way?

After a Shelter Experience | Use the following prompts to invite children to talk about their shelter experiences.

- Did you and your family have to find a different place to live?
- Did you feel the way Andrew feels in the story?
- Can you tell a story about anything you saw at the shelter?

ART CENTER OPTIONS

For 5- to 8-Year-Olds

- Draw a picture or map of your home or an airport.
- Draw a picture of a grown-up in your family who takes care of you.

After a Storm and a Shelter Experience

- Draw a picture of how or where your family found a shelter after our disaster.
- Draw a picture of someone you met at the shelter.

WRITING CENTER OPTIONS

For 5- to 8-Year-Olds

- Dictate or write a sentence or story to go with your picture.
- Dictate or write a sentence or story about where you and your family went after our disaster.

FOOTPRINTS IN THE SNOW

**BY CYNTHIA BENJAMIN
AND JACQUELINE ROGERS
(ILLUSTRATOR)**

We follow the tracks of different animals through the snow back to their cozy homes.

APPROPRIATE FOR:

Earthquakes
Emotional Resilience
Epidemics and Mass Casualty
   Incidents
Fires and Explosions
Floods
Hurricanes
▶ **Shelter Experiences**
▶ **Tornadoes and Major
   Storms**
Volcanic Eruptions

DISCUSSION STARTERS

Use the following prompts to encourage the children to talk about their experiences, either in the context of the book or in the context of a traumatic experience.

For 5- to 8-Year-Olds

- Have you ever seen snow? If you have, how did it feel? If you haven't, how do you think it would feel?
- Have you ever hurried home through the snow?

> **After a Shelter Experience |** Use the following prompts to invite children to talk about their shelter experiences.
> - Did you and your family have to find a different place to go in our big storm?
> - Were you glad to have a place inside where it was warm?
> - Did you wish you could be in your own home?

ART CENTER OPTIONS

For 2- to 8-Year-Olds

- Press handprints in playdough.
- Trace your footprints on paper.
- Draw a picture of an animal in the snow.

For 5- to 8-Year-Olds

- Draw a picture or map of how you go to your house.
- Use white chalk on dark construction paper to draw a snowy or stormy scene.

> **After a Storm and a Shelter Experience**
> - Draw a picture of how or where your family found a shelter in our big storm.

WRITING CENTER OPTIONS

For 3- to 8-Year-Olds

- Dictate or write a sentence or story to go with your picture.
- Dictate or write a sentence or story about where you and your family went in our big storm.

FRANKLIN AND THE THUNDER-STORM

BY PAULETTE BOURGEOIS AND BRENDA CLARK (ILLUSTRATOR)

Franklin Tortoise is afraid of thunderstorms. When a big storm comes up, his friends Hawk, Beaver, Fox, and Owl all have different ways to help him understand and cope with it.

APPROPRIATE FOR:
Earthquakes
▶ **Emotional Resilience**
Epidemics and Mass Casualty
    Incidents
Fires and Explosions
▶ **Floods**
▶ **Hurricanes**
▶ **Shelter Experiences**
Tornadoes and Major Storms
Volcanic Eruptions

DISCUSSION STARTERS

Use the following prompts to encourage the children to talk about their experiences, either in the context of the book or in the context of a traumatic experience.

For 3- to 8-Year-Olds
- Let's look at all of the different animals in the book.
- Which animals can you name?
- Did you ever play with a flashlight when the lights went off? What did you do with the flashlight?
- Did the lights go off where you were during our big storm? If so, were they off for a long time? What did you and your family do?

For 5- to 8-Year-Olds
- Fox's mother took care of Franklin during the storm.
- Where was Franklin's mother?
- Did you ever have someone else's mother take care of you when you were scared?
- Did you feel scared during our big storm?
- Franklin and his friends talked about the storm.
- Do you ever talk about our big storm with your friends?

After a Shelter Experience | Use the following prompts to invite children to talk about their shelter experiences.
- Was Fox's house like a shelter?
- When you stayed at a shelter, did grown-ups you didn't know take care of you?
- How did that make you feel?

ART CENTER OPTIONS

For 3- to 8-Year-Olds
- Draw one of the animals in the story of Franklin and the thunderstorm.
- Draw a picture of a time when someone else's mother (or father) took care of you when you were scared.

After a Shelter Experience
- Draw a picture of the time when you stayed at a shelter.

Extended Project
- Work in a group to draw a big picture of a shelter after our big storm.

WRITING CENTER OPTIONS

For 3- to 8-Year-Olds
- Dictate or write a sentence or story to go with your picture.

GO AWAY, BIG GREEN MONSTER!

BY ED EMBERLEY

A book with die-cut pages so the child-reader can first construct then deconstruct a "big green monster." A classic to help young children with active imaginations cope with their scary thoughts.

APPROPRIATE FOR:

Earthquakes

▶ **Emotional Resilience**

Epidemics and Mass Casualty
  Incidents

Fires and Explosions

Floods

Hurricanes

Shelter Experiences

Tornadoes and Major Storms

Volcanic Eruptions

DISCUSSION STARTERS

Use the following prompts to encourage the children to talk about their experiences, either in the context of the book or in the context of a traumatic experience.

For 3- to 8-Year-Olds

- Are big, green monsters real or "pretend"?
- Are you ever afraid of something even though it's not real? Why?
- Are you ever afraid of something that is real? Like what?
- What can you do when you are afraid of something?
- Can you ask a grown-up to help you?
- Can grown-ups protect you from things that are not real?
- Can grown-ups protect you from things that are real?
- Name some grown-ups who can help you if you are afraid of something.

ART CENTER OPTIONS

For 3- to 8-Year-Olds

- Cut out magazine pictures of faces.
- Draw a picture of something scary that is not real.
- Draw a picture of something scary that is real.
- Draw a picture of a grown-up who can help you when you are afraid of something.

WRITING CENTER OPTIONS

For 3- to 8-Year-Olds

- Dictate or write a label such as "scary" or "nice" for your cut-out face.
- Dictate or write a sentence or story to go with your picture.

THE GROUCHY LADYBUG

BY ERIC CARLE

A grouchy ladybug tries to pick a fight with each of a series of increasingly large animals. Each animal reluctantly agrees to fight, but the ladybug flies on, searching for yet another creature to challenge. At the beginning and end of the story, a sympathetic ladybug offers the grouchy ladybug a meal.

APPROPRIATE FOR:

Earthquakes
▶ **Emotional Resilience**
Epidemics and Mass Casualty
    Incidents
Fires and Explosions
Floods
Hurricanes
Shelter Experiences
Tornadoes and Major Storms
Volcanic Eruptions

DISCUSSION STARTERS

Use the following prompts to encourage the children to talk about their experiences, either in the context of the book or in the context of a traumatic experience.

For 5- to 8-Year-Olds

■ Would a ladybug really try to fight with a whale?
■ Why did the ladybug in the story want to fight with so many animals? How did he feel? Could something bad have happened to the ladybug to make him feel grouchy?
■ Have you ever felt that way? Did you ever want to fight with someone else because you felt that way?
■ What did the other ladybug do? Can we help our friends when they feel grouchy?

ART CENTER OPTIONS

For 5- to 8-Year-Olds

■ Make pictures of ladybugs with crayons, paint, or other materials.
■ Look through magazines for pictures of persons with grouchy expressions and make a "Grouchy Collage."

WRITING CENTER OPTIONS

For 5- to 8-Year-Olds

■ Dictate or write a label such as "grouchy" or "nice" for your ladybug.
■ Dictate or write a sentence or story to go with your picture.
■ Dictate or write a sentence or story about grouchy people to go with the collage.

A HOUSE OF LEAVES

**BY SOYA KIYOSHI AND
AKIKO HAYASHI
(ILLUSTRATOR)**

A gentle tale of a child who is waiting out a shower under a leafy shrub. Insects join her, one by one. "We're a family!" she laughs.

APPROPRIATE FOR:

Earthquakes
Emotional Resilience
Epidemics and Mass Casualty
  Incidents
Fires and Explosions
Floods
Hurricanes
▶ **Shelter Experiences**
▶ **Tornadoes and Major
    Storms**
Volcanic Eruptions

DISCUSSION STARTERS

Use the following prompts to encourage the children to talk about their experiences, either in the context of the book or in the context of a traumatic experience.

For 5- to 8-Year-Olds

- Was it raining very hard when Sarah looked for a shelter?
- What about in our big storm—did it rain here as hard as it did in this book?
- Did the rain come down harder in our big storm?
- What happened to your real house in our big storm?

After a Shelter Experience | Use the following prompts to invite children to talk about their shelter experiences.

- Did you stay in a shelter during our big storm?
- Did you see some strange insects at the shelter?
- What about people? Did you see any strange people at the shelter?
- Did you feel that the other people at the shelter were your family?
- Did you get to go back to your real house after our big storm?

ART CENTER OPTIONS

For 3- to 5-Year-Olds

- Use glue with pipe cleaners, buttons, fabric scraps, paper, or boxes to make a shelter of "leaves."
- Draw a picture of what you did in our big storm.
- Draw a picture of the shelter you went to in our big storm.
- Draw a picture of your house after our big storm.

For 5- to 8-Year-Olds

- Draw a picture of a funny insect.
- Draw a picture of yourself.

WRITING CENTER OPTIONS

For 3- to 8-Year-Olds

- Dictate or write a sentence or story to go with your picture or shelter creation.

I REMEMBER MISS PERRY

BY PAT BRISSON AND STEPHANE JORISCH (ILLUSTRATOR)

This is a delicate story about painful loss in a real-life setting. A beloved teacher is killed in a car accident. Caring adults help the children talk and remember Miss Perry together.

APPROPRIATE FOR:

Earthquakes

Emotional Resilience

▶ **Epidemics and Mass Casualty Incidents**

Fires and Explosions

Floods

Hurricanes

Shelter Experiences

Tornadoes and Major Storms

Volcanic Eruptions

DISCUSSION STARTERS

Use the following prompts to encourage the children to talk about their experiences, either in the context of the book or in the context of a traumatic experience.

For 3- to 8-Year-Olds

- What happened to Miss Perry in the story?
- How did the children feel when Miss Perry died?
- Do you know anyone who has died in our epidemic (or other disaster)?
- How does his (or her) death make you feel? Why?
- What is your fondest wish for today?

For 5- to 8-Year-Olds

- Who is Ms. Jackson?
- What did Ms. Jackson do in the story?
- Did anyone like Ms. Jackson help you think about how you feel?

ART CENTER OPTIONS

For 3- to 8-Year-Olds

- Draw a picture of a teacher or someone else you remember.
- Draw a picture of your fondest wish for today.

WRITING CENTER OPTIONS

For 3- to 8-Year-Olds

- Dictate or write a sentence or story about your picture.
- Dictate or write a sentence or story about someone who died.
- Dictate or write a sentence or story about how you feel about someone who died.

IF FROGS MADE THE WEATHER

BY MARION DANE BAUER AND DOROTHY DONOHUE (ILLUSTRATOR)

If frogs made the weather, we would always have rain. If polar bears made the weather, we would always have snow. Animals cope with storms in different ways.

APPROPRIATE FOR:

Earthquakes
Emotional Resilience
Epidemics and Mass Casualty
    Incidents
Fires and Explosions
Floods
Hurricanes
Shelter Experiences
▶ **Tornadoes and Major
    Storms**
Volcanic Eruptions

DISCUSSION STARTERS

Use the following prompts to encourage the children to talk about their experiences, either in the context of the book or in the context of a traumatic experience.

For 2- to 8-Year-Olds

- Can you see the boy looking at animals in the pictures? What is he seeing?
- Do you think frogs liked our big storm?'
- Do you think turtles liked our big storm?
- The turtles snapped their shells shut for shelter from the storm. Did your family shut your doors and stay inside during our big storm?
- Did you smile in the dry dark? Why?
- Did you snuggle in someone's lap? If you did, how did that feel?
- Did you hear the thunder roar? If you did, how did that feel?
- Did you hear the drip, drip, drip? If you did, how did that sound?

For 5- to 8-Year-Olds

- Look at Dorothy Donohue's pictures:
    - ❏ She cut pieces of paper to glue on her picture.
    - ❏ She used a rubber stamp to make white flowers on a wall.
    - ❏ She scratched lines in wet green paint to make a grassy field below the hawk.

ART CENTER OPTIONS

For 3- to 8-Year-Olds

- Draw a picture of what you did in our _____ (insert the appropriate term, for example, "big storm").
- Draw a picture of snuggling in someone's lap when you are afraid.
- Use fingerpaint to make a picture of your yard after the storm.

For 5- to 8-Year-Olds

- Try one of Dorothy Donohue's art techniques:
    - ❏ Cut pieces of paper to glue on a picture.
    - ❏ Use a rubber stamp to make a background.
    - ❏ Scratch lines in wet paint to show texture.

WRITING CENTER OPTIONS

For 3- to 8-Year-Olds

- Dictate or write a sentence or story to go with your picture.

"I'M NOT SCARED!"

BY JONATHAN ALLEN

Baby Owl goes out in the woods at night. He says he's not scared—after all, staying out at night is what owls do! But it's pretty scary. His father is reassuring, telling him, "It's OK to be a little scared of the dark."

APPROPRIATE FOR:
▶ **Earthquakes**
▶ **Emotional Resilience**
▶ **Epidemics and Mass Casualty Incidents**
   Fires and Explosions
▶ **Floods**
▶ **Hurricanes**
   Shelter Experiences
▶ **Tornadoes and Major Storms**
   Volcanic Eruptions

DISCUSSION STARTERS

Use the following prompts to encourage the children to talk about their experiences, either in the context of the book or in the context of a traumatic experience.

For 2- to 8-Year-Olds
- Baby Owl has a toy baby owl named Owly.
- Do you have a toy baby like Owly? What does your toy baby look like?
- Do you ever think your toy baby might feel scared?
- What did Baby Owl's Papa do? He gave Baby Owl a hug and tucked him in bed; does your father ever do that? What about your mother or grandmother or aunt?
- How do you feel when one of them does that?
- Papa Owl read Baby Owl's favorite story to him.
- Does anyone read stories to you? Do you have a favorite bedtime story?
- Does that make you feel safe?

For 3- to 8-Year-Olds
- What animals does Baby Owl meet in the woods?
- Was Baby Owl scared of the other animals? Why was he scared?
- How else did he feel?
- Do you ever feel mad about feeling scared? Why?

After a Traumatic Experience | Use the following prompt to invite children to talk about their experiences.
- When you were scared during our _____ (insert the appropriate term, such as flood or other disaster), did you find out that grown-ups would take care of you?

ART CENTER OPTIONS

For 3- to 8-Year-Olds
- Draw a picture of your toy baby.
- Draw a picture of Baby Owl and Owly.
- Draw a picture of a time when you felt scared and someone helped you.

WRITING CENTER OPTIONS

For 3- to 8-Year-Olds
- Dictate or write a sentence or story to go with your picture.
- Dictate or write a letter to someone about when he or she reads to you:

"I feel safe when you read to me at bedtime. My favorite book is _____."

IN THE MIDDLE OF THE PUDDLE

BY MIKE THALER AND BRUCE DEGEN (ILLUSTRATOR)

Frog and turtle are sitting in the middle of their puddle as the rain makes it as big as an ocean. Finally, the sun comes out and returns things to normal.

Note: At the time we prepared these activities, this book was available in only 409 public libraries nationwide, less than our standard of 500. However, we include it here because the illustrations can help young children comprehend floods and because it can prompt children's discussions of rescue experiences.

APPROPRIATE FOR:

Earthquakes
Emotional Resilience
Epidemics and Mass Casualty
    Incidents
Fires and Explosions
▶ **Floods**
Hurricanes
Shelter Experiences
Tornadoes and Major Storms
Volcanic Eruptions

DISCUSSION STARTERS

Use the following prompts to encourage the children to talk about their experiences, either in the context of the book or in the context of a traumatic experience.

For 2- to 8-Year-Olds

- Fred and Ted wished the rain would stop. Did you wish the rain would stop when we had our flood?
- How did our flood turn a puddle into a pond?
- How did our flood turn a pond into a lake?
- Did our flood turn a lake into a sea? Why?
- What happened to your home in our flood?

> **After a Rescue Experience** | Use the following prompts to invite children to talk about their rescue experiences.
> - Did you see any boats in our flood? How did people use boats to help others?
> - Did someone come in a boat to rescue you? How did they find you?
> - Did you like riding in the boat? Why?

ART CENTER OPTIONS

For 3- to 8-Year-Olds

- Draw a picture of what you saw after our flood.
- Cut out magazine pictures that show how our town looked when the floodwaters went down.

WRITING CENTER OPTIONS

For 3- to 8-Year-Olds

- Dictate or write a sentence or story about your picture.

For 5- to 8-Year-Olds

- Dictate or write a list of ways people can get bugs, frogs, turtles, and other animals out of their houses after a flood.

IT'S MINE!

BY LEO LIONNI

Three young frogs spend a lot of time arguing and bickering with each other. When a real crisis comes, they realize that cooperation makes more sense than arguing.

APPROPRIATE FOR:

Earthquakes
Emotional Resilience
Epidemics and Mass Casualty
    Incidents
Fires and Explosions
▶ **Floods**
▶ **Hurricanes**
▶ **Shelter Experiences**
▶ **Tornadoes and Major**
    Storms
Volcanic Eruptions

DISCUSSION STARTERS

Use the following prompts to encourage the children to talk about their experiences, either in the context of the book or in the context of a traumatic experience.

For 3- to 8-Year-Olds
- Were the frogs friends?
- How do you know the frogs were friends?

For 5- to 8-Year-Olds
- What was the frogs' shelter in the storm? How did it keep them safe?
- Who protected the frogs from the rising water? How did they do that?
- Where did you stay in our hurricane (or other disaster)? Did you feel safe?
- Look at Leo Lionni's artwork:
    - The animals, rocks, and plants look like cut paper.
    - Some of the cut paper has paintbrush strokes on it.

ART CENTER OPTIONS

For 3- to 8-Year-Olds
- Experiment with cut paper pictures.

For 5- to 8-Year-Olds
- Make a picture using Leo Lionni's technique.

> **After a Rescue or Shelter Experience** | Use the following prompt to invite children to talk about their rescue experiences.
> - Draw a picture of how you were rescued.

WRITING CENTER OPTIONS

For 3- to 8-Year-Olds
- Dictate or write a sentence or story about how you made your picture.
- Dictate or write a sentence or story about our storm (or other disaster).

For 5- to 8-Year-Olds
- Dictate or write a list of ways people can be rescued.

> **After a Rescue or Shelter Experience** | **For 5- to 8-Year-Olds**
> - Dictate or write a sentence or story about when you were rescued in our hurricane (or other disaster).
> - Dictate or write a letter to someone who rescued or sheltered you.
> - Pretend you are being interviewed on television. Dictate or write three things you would tell a news reporter about being rescued.

JUST YOU AND ME

BY SAM MCBRATNEY AND IVAN BATES (ILLUSTRATOR)

Big Gander Goose and Little Goosey are looking for shelter from a storm. Little Goosey doesn't want to be with anyone except Gander. Will they be able to find a safe space to share?

APPROPRIATE FOR:

Earthquakes

Emotional Resilience

Epidemics and Mass Casualty Incidents

Fires and Explosions

▶ **Floods**

▶ **Hurricanes**

▶ **Shelter Experiences**

▶ **Tornadoes and Major Storms**

Volcanic Eruptions

DISCUSSION STARTERS

Use the following prompts to encourage the children to talk about their experiences, either in the context of the book or in the context of a traumatic experience.

For 3- to 8-Year-Olds

- What did Little Goosey want?
- What did Gander Goose do?
- Where did Gander Goose and Little Goosey decide to stay during the storm? Why did they decide to stay there?
- Did Little Goosey decide it was okay for the other animals to stay with them?
- Did you and your family go somewhere safe before our storm (or hurricane)? Where did you go?

After a Shelter Experience | Use the following prompts to invite children to talk about their shelter experiences.

- Did you stay in a shelter during our storm (or hurricane)? What did it look like?
- Was your father or mother with you?
- Did other people stay with you in the shelter?
- How was the shelter different from home? How did you feel about that?

ART CENTER OPTIONS

For 3- to 8-Year-Olds

- Draw a picture of Little Goosey and Gander Goose.
- Draw a picture about a time when a grown-up helped you stay safe.
- Draw a picture of how you think someone who is safe looks.
- With a partner, use playdough, craft sticks, or other materials to make a shelter with a doorway and a roof.

WRITING CENTER OPTIONS

For 3- to 8-Year-Olds

- Dictate or write a sentence or story to go with your picture.
- Dictate or write a letter to your mother, father, or grandparent about a time when she or he helped you stay safe.
- Dictate or write a list of three rules a shelter should have so everyone can get along together.

After a Shelter Experience

- Dictate or write a letter to someone who helped you stay safe in our storm (or hurricane).

THE LITTLE FIRE ENGINE

BY LOIS LENSKI

Fireman Small and his little red fire engine put out the fire and rescue a young girl.

APPROPRIATE FOR:

Earthquakes
Emotional Resilience
Epidemics and Mass Casualty
   Incidents
▶ **Fires and Explosions**
Floods
Hurricanes
Shelter Experiences
Tornadoes and Major Storms
▶ **Volcanic Eruptions**

DISCUSSION STARTERS

Use the following prompts to encourage the children to talk about their experiences, either in the context of the book or in the context of a traumatic experience.

For 3- to 8-Year-Olds

- Did you see fire trucks when we had our fire (or other disaster)?
- Why did the firefighters need trucks to do their jobs?

For 5- to 8-Year-Olds

- Did you notice the hose, hydrant, water, or ladder when we had our fire? What did firefighters do with those?
- If you were a firefighter, what would you tell people to do in a fire?

ART CENTER OPTIONS

For 3- to 8-Year-Olds

- Draw a picture of a fire truck.
- Draw a picture of what firefighters did during our fire (or other disaster).

WRITING CENTER OPTIONS

For 3- to 8-Year-Olds

- Dictate or write a sentence or story to go with your picture.
- Dictate or write a sentence or story about our fire (or other disaster).

MISS BINDERGARTEN STAYS HOME FROM KINDERGARTEN

BY JOSEPH SLATE AND ASHLEY WOLFF (ILLUSTRATOR)

Miss Bindergarten gets the flu and has to stay home. It's hard to have a teacher you don't know.

APPROPRIATE FOR:
Earthquakes
Emotional Resilience
▶ **Epidemics and Mass Casualty Incidents**
Fires and Explosions
Floods
Hurricanes
Shelter Experiences
Tornadoes and Major Storms
Volcanic Eruptions

DISCUSSION STARTERS

Use the following prompts to encourage the children to talk about their experiences, either in the context of the book or in the context of a traumatic experience.

For 3- to 8-Year-Olds
- Let's look at the illustrations. Who takes care of Miss Bindergarten when she's sick?
- Who takes care of Franny? Who takes care of Lenny?
- Who gets sick at the end of the story? Why?
- How is their classroom like our classroom?
- What does the word "epidemic" mean?
- Who in our classroom has gotten sick?
- How is their classroom different from our classroom?
- Has everyone who has gotten sick in our class come back to school?

ART CENTER OPTIONS

For 3- to 8-Year-Olds
- Draw a picture of someone in our class who was sick.
- Draw a picture for a get-well card for someone who is sick.

Extended Projects
- Draw a picture for a class book about our epidemic.
- Draw a picture for a classroom exhibit about our epidemic.

WRITING CENTER OPTIONS

For 3- to 8-Year-Olds
- Dictate or write a sentence or a story about someone in our class who was sick.
- Dictate or write a message for a get-well card for someone who is sick.

Extended Projects
- Dictate or write a sentence or story for a class book about our epidemic.
- Dictate or write a sentence or story for a classroom exhibit about our epidemic.

MOMMY, CARRY ME PLEASE!

BY JANE CABRERA

Every kind of mother animal has a special way to carry her babies.

APPROPRIATE FOR:

Earthquakes
▸ **Emotional Resilience**
Epidemics and Mass Casualty
Incidents
Fires and Explosions
▸ **Floods**
▸ **Hurricanes**
▸ **Shelter Experiences**
▸ **Tornadoes and Major**
Storms
Volcanic Eruptions

DISCUSSION STARTERS

Use the following prompts to encourage the children to talk about their experiences, either in the context of the book or in the context of a traumatic experience.

For 2- to 8-Year-Olds

- Baby animals like it when their mothers carry them. Did you like to be carried when you were a baby?
- Do you ever carry a doll around?
- Do you still like to be carried sometimes?
- Can you think of a time when your mother, father, or another grown-up carried you?
  - When you were tired?
  - Lonely?
  - Scared?
- Did you feel better when someone carried you? Why did you feel better?
- What about when a grown-up holds you or sits beside you?
- Can you think of some ways that grown-ups make us feel safe?
- Did any grown-ups make you feel safe during our big storm?

For 5- to 8-Year-Olds

- Look at Jane Cabrera's artwork:
  - The backgrounds look like finger-painting.
  - She used wide brushes to paint orange, white, and other colors.
  - She used a narrow brush to draw eyes, noses, and black edges.

ART CENTER OPTIONS

For 3- to 8-Year-Olds

- Draw a picture about a time when a grown-up carried you.
- Draw a picture about a time when a grown-up made you feel safe.

For 5- to 8-Year-Olds

- Experiment with Jane Cabrera's art techniques:
  - Use finger-painting.
  - Use wide brushes and paint.
  - Use narrow brushes and paint.

WRITING CENTER OPTIONS

For 3- to 8-Year-Olds

- Dictate or write a sentence or story about a time when a grown-up carried you.
- Dictate or write a sentence or story about a time when a grown-up made you feel safe.

For 5- to 8-Year-Olds

- Dictate or write a sentence or story about how you painted your picture.

THE OWL AND THE WOODPECKER

BY BRIAN WILDSMITH

Woodpecker makes a lot of noise during the day when Owl is trying to sleep. Their relationship is not a friendly one. But everything changes when Woodpecker saves Owl from danger.

APPROPRIATE FOR:

Earthquakes
Emotional Resilience
Epidemics and Mass Casualty Incidents
Fires and Explosions
Floods
Hurricanes
▶ **Shelter Experiences**
▶ **Tornadoes and Major Storms**
Volcanic Eruptions

DISCUSSION STARTERS

Use the following prompts to encourage the children to talk about their experiences, either in the context of the book or in the context of a traumatic experience.

For 3- to 8-Year-Olds

- Were the woodpecker and the owl friends in the beginning? Why?
- Why and how did they become friends?
- What happened to the owl's house?
- Did our big storm blow your house down?
- Where did your family go after that?

For 5- to 8-Year-Olds

- Look at Brian Wildsmith's illustrations:
  - ❑ He made cut-paper collages.
  - ❑ He used finger-painting.
  - ❑ He used tools to make patterns in the wet paint.
  - ❑ He used brush strokes to paint on the paper.
  - ❑ He used brushes to dab paint on the paper.

After a Shelter Experience | Use the following prompt to invite children to talk about their shelter experiences.
- Did you make any new friends at the shelter? If so, how?

ART CENTER OPTIONS

For 3- to 8-Year-Olds

- Draw a picture of how the sky looked during our storm.

For 5- to 8-Year-Olds

- Make a picture using one of Brian Wildsmith's techniques:
  - ❑ Cut paper collages or paint with fingerpaints. Use tools to make patterns in the wet paint. Use brush strokes to paint on the paper. Use brushes to dab paint on the paper.

Extended Projects

- Experiment with two or more of Brian Wildsmith's art techniques.
- Combine the artwork and stories about our storm in a class exhibit.

WRITING CENTER OPTIONS

For 3- to 8-Year-Olds

- Dictate or write a sentence or story to go with your picture.

For 5- to 8-Year-Olds

- Dictate or write a label or text panel for a classroom exhibit about our storm.

POLICEMAN LOU AND POLICEWOMAN SUE

BY LISA DESIMINI

A day in the life of two police officers in a small town, showing all the ways they work to keep everyone safe.

APPROPRIATE FOR:

Earthquakes
Emotional Resilience
Epidemics and Mass Casualty Incidents
Fires and Explosions
Floods
Hurricanes
Shelter Experiences
▶ **Tornadoes and Major Storms**
Volcanic Eruptions

DISCUSSION STARTERS

Use the following prompts to encourage the children to talk about their experiences, either in the context of the book or in the context of a traumatic experience.

For 3- to 8-Year-Olds

- What do Policeman Lou and Policewoman Sue do?
- Does our school have a crossing guard? What does she (or he) do?
- Does our neighborhood have any police officers who help people?

For 5- to 8-Year-Olds

- Can you think of a time when a police officer helped someone?
- Look at how Lisa Desimini used brushes to paint patterns:
  - She painted lines on windows, sidewalks, streets, floors, and the crossing guard's vest.
  - She painted stripes on shirts and curtains.
  - She painted checkerboards on curtains and floors.

> **After a Rescue Experience** | Use the following prompt to invite children to talk about their experiences.
> - How did police officers rescue people in our big storm?

ART CENTER OPTIONS

For 3- to 8-Year-Olds

- Draw a picture of a police officer.
- Draw a picture of a time when someone rescued you or someone in your family.

For 5- to 8-Year-Olds

- Experiment with Lisa Desimini's art technique:
  - Use brushes to paint lines.
  - Use brushes to paint stripes.
  - Use brushes to paint checkerboards.

WRITING CENTER OPTIONS

For 3- to 8-Year-Olds

- Dictate or write a sentence or story about a police officer.
- Dictate or write a sentence or story about a time when someone rescued you or someone in your family.

For 5- to 8-Year-Olds

- Dictate or write a sentence or story about how you made your picture.

RAIN

BY PETER SPIER

A brother and sister play joyfully in the rain in this wordless picture book.

APPROPRIATE FOR:

Earthquakes
Emotional Resilience
Epidemics and Mass Casualty
    Incidents
Fires and Explosions
Floods
Hurricanes
Shelter Experiences
▶ **Tornadoes and Major**
    Storms
Volcanic Eruptions

DISCUSSION STARTERS

Use the following prompts to encourage the children to talk about their experiences, either in the context of the book or in the context of a traumatic experience.

For 5- to 8-Year-Olds

- Are these pictures anything like our big storm? Why?
- Do most of the pictures show ordinary rain?
- One picture shows a very windy storm. Does that picture look similar to our big storm?
- Did you see anyone running through the rain and wind in our big storm?
- Did their clothes blow behind them? Did their umbrellas turn inside out?

After a Shelter Experience | Use the following prompts to invite children to talk about their shelter experiences.

- The family in these pictures stayed at home during the rain. Did you get to stay at home during our big storm? What did you do while it was raining?
- If you went to a shelter, did you play like these children?
- Did you eat like these children? What was one of the favorite things you ate?
- Did you sleep in a bed like these children? What did your bed look like?
- Did you like staying in a shelter the way these children liked staying at home during the rain?

ART CENTER OPTIONS

For 3- to 5-Year-Olds

- Draw a picture of one thing you did in our big storm.
- Draw a picture of part of the shelter you went to in our big storm.
- Draw a picture of your house after our big storm. Then draw a picture that shows how it should look when it is repaired.

For 5- to 8-Year-Olds

- Draw a picture of yourself in the rain.

WRITING CENTER OPTIONS

For 3- to 5-Year-Olds

- Dictate or write a sentence or story to go with your picture.
- Dictate or write a list of things that will be needed to repair your house.

RHINOS WHO RESCUE

BY JULIE MAMMANO

The rhinos are firefighters in this exciting picture book filled with adventurous rescues and firefighting vocabulary.

Note: At the time we prepared these activities, this book was available in only 436 public libraries nationwide, less than our standard of 500. However, we include it here because it depicts rescuers in a variety of disaster situations, making it a versatile resource.

APPROPRIATE FOR:
Earthquakes
Emotional Resilience
Epidemics and Mass Casualty Incidents
▶ **Fires and Explosions**
Floods
Hurricanes
Shelter Experiences
Tornadoes and Major Storms
Volcanic Eruptions

DISCUSSION STARTERS

Use the following prompts to encourage the children to talk about their experiences, either in the context of the book or in the context of a traumatic experience.

For 2- to 8-Year-Olds
- Are rhinos really rescuers? Why?
- Did you see any real rescuers in our storm? What did they look like?
- What were the rescuers doing?
  - Did they go out in a boat to rescue someone? When would they use a boat?
  - Did they reach down from a helicopter to rescue someone? When would they use a helicopter?

For 5- to 8-Year-Olds
- Look at Julie Mammano's pictures:
  - Do you see shapes in her pictures?
  - Do you see patterns in her pictures?

> **After a Rescue Experience |** Use the following prompts to invite children to talk about their rescue experiences.
> - When you were scared during our flood, how did grown-ups take care of you?
> - Did firefighters rescue you like the rhinos rescued the rabbits?
> - How are the firefighters and rhinos alike?

ART CENTER OPTIONS

For 3- to 8-Year-Olds
- Draw a picture of a rescuer.
- Draw a picture of our flood.

For 5- to 8-Year-Olds
- Draw a picture with shapes in it.
- Draw a picture with a pattern in it.

WRITING CENTER OPTIONS

For 3- to 8-Year-Olds
- Dictate or write a sentence or story to go with your picture.
- Dictate or write a letter to someone who took care of you in our flood.

RIVER FRIENDLY, RIVER WILD

BY JANE KURTZ AND NEIL BRENNAN (ILLUSTRATOR)

The story of the Red River flood of 1997, told in poetic language from the point of view of a young girl and her family who evacuated their home.

APPROPRIATE FOR:

Earthquakes
Emotional Resilience
Epidemics and Mass Casualty
Incidents
Fires and Explosions
▶ **Floods**
Hurricanes
▶ **Shelter Experiences**
Tornadoes and Major Storms
Volcanic Eruptions

DISCUSSION STARTERS

Use the following prompts to encourage the children to talk about their experiences, either in the context of the book or in the context of a traumatic experience.

For 5- to 8-Year-Olds

- Did our flood look like the flood in these pictures?
- Did you see a pile of sandbags during our flood? What do you think the sandbags were for? Do you think the sandbags were heavy?
- Did any buildings burn in our flood? Why do you think they burned?

After an Evacuation Experience | Use the following prompts to invite children to talk about their evacuation experiences.

- Did you pack a suitcase when your family was evacuated? If so, what did you put in it?
- Was your family able to go back home?
- How was your house different when you went back to it?

After a Shelter Experience | Use the following prompts to invite children to talk about their shelter experiences.

- Did you see a Red Cross truck? What did the Red Cross workers do to help people?
- What did you like about staying with strangers at your shelter?
- What was not so nice?

ART CENTER OPTIONS

For 3- to 8-Year-Olds

- Draw a picture of your house before the flood.
- Draw a picture of your house after the flood.
- Draw a picture of something that happened during the flood.

WRITING CENTER OPTIONS

For 3- to 8-Year-Olds

- Dictate or write a list of things you would take to a shelter.
- Dictate or write a sentence or story to go with your picture.

Sam Is Never Scared

BY THIERRY ROBBERECHT AND PHILIPPE GOOSSENS (ILLUSTRATOR)

Sam is usually very brave with his friends, but he does get scared sometimes. He doesn't want to be called a scaredy-cat. Sam's dad helps him cope with being scared.

APPROPRIATE FOR:

Earthquakes
▶ **Emotional Resilience**
▶ **Epidemics and Mass Casualt Incidents**
Fires and Explosions
▶ **Floods**
Hurricanes
Shelter Experiences
▶ **Tornadoes and Major Storms**
Volcanic Eruptions

DISCUSSION STARTERS

Use the following prompts to encourage the children to talk about their experiences, either in the context of the book or in the context of a traumatic experience.

For 3- to 8-Year-Olds

- Was Sam scared of something?
- What made Sam feel scared?
- What kinds of things make you feel scared?
- How does "scared" feel?
- Did Sam find out that everyone is scared of something?
- What was Sam's dad afraid of when he was Sam's age?
- What did Sam's dad do?
- Did your father, mother, or grandmother ever talk with you about something that makes you feel scared? How did they help you?
- Do you think your favorite grown-up is afraid of something? What?

> **After a Traumatic Experience |** Use the following prompts to invite children to talk about their experiences.
> - Did you feel scared during our storm (or other disaster)? What made you feel less scared?
> - Did anyone help you feel less scared?
> - Do you think everyone needs help when they feel scared?

ART CENTER OPTIONS

For 3- to 8-Year-Olds

- Draw a picture of a time when you were scared.
- Draw a picture of a time during our storm (or other disaster) when you were scared.
- Draw a picture of a time when you were not scared.

WRITING CENTER OPTIONS

For 3- to 8-Year-Olds

- Dictate or write a sentence or story to go with your picture.
- It is okay to feel scared sometimes. Write or dictate some words you can use to talk yourself out of being scared, like "I am going to be just fine."
- Dictate or write a letter to someone who helps you when you feel scared:

"Dear _____: You help me when I feel scared because you _____."

A Shelter in Our Car

BY MONICA GUNNING AND ELAINE PEDLAR (ILLUSTRATOR)

Zettie and her mother find themselves homeless after Zettie's father dies. Mama is resourceful, and they live in their car while Mama looks for a job and Zettie goes to school.

Note: At the time we prepared these activities, this book was available in only 400 public libraries nationwide, less than our standard of 500. However, we include it here because it is an excellent book for exploring the subject of homelessness, a very common issue for families that experience disasters.

APPROPRIATE FOR:

Earthquakes
Emotional Resilience
Epidemics and Mass Casualty
  Incidents
Fires and Explosions
▶ **Floods**
▶ **Hurricanes**
▶ **Shelter Experiences**
▶ **Tornadoes and Major**
    Storms
Volcanic Eruptions

DISCUSSION STARTERS

Use the following prompts to encourage the children to talk about their experiences, either in the context of the book or in the context of a traumatic experience.

For 3- to 8-Year-Olds

- What is this story about?
- Do you know anyone who lost his house in our hurricane?
- Did you ever have to sleep in a shelter or in your car?

For 4- to 5-Year-Olds

- Did you ever see someone sleeping in a park?
- Why do you think they were doing that?
- Look at Elaine Pedlar's pictures:
  - She uses pastels.
  - She puts one color on top of another.

After a Shelter Experience | Use the following prompt to invite children to talk about their shelter experiences.
- If you stayed in a shelter, did you like the shelter or did you feel like Zettie?

ART CENTER OPTIONS

For 3- to 8-Year-Olds

- Experiment with pastels on white and colored paper.

For 5- to 8-Year-Olds

- Make a picture using Elaine Pedlar's art technique.

After a Shelter Experience | For 3- to 8-Year-Olds
- Draw a picture about the time you slept in a shelter or in your car.
- Draw a picture about when your family was able to go back home.

WRITING CENTER OPTIONS

For 3- to 8-Year-Olds

- Dictate or write a sentence or story about how you think you would feel if your family had to live in a car.

For 5- to 8-Year-Olds

- Dictate or write a sentence or story about how you made your picture.

After a Shelter Experience
- Dictate or write a sentence or story about a time when you slept in a shelter or in your car, or about how you felt when your family was able to go back home.

THE SNOWY DAY

BY EZRA JACK KEATS

A young boy observes his urban neighborhood after an overnight blizzard. His observations help him feel mastery of an unfamiliar situation.

APPROPRIATE FOR:

Earthquakes
Emotional Resilience
Epidemics and Mass Casualty
  Incidents
Fires and Explosions
Floods
Hurricanes
Shelter Experiences
▶ **Tornadoes and Major
  Storms**
Volcanic Eruptions

DISCUSSION STARTERS

Use the following prompts to encourage the children to talk about their experiences, either in the context of the book or in the context of a traumatic experience.

For 2- to 8-Year-Olds

- What did the boy see when he woke up?
- Were you ever surprised to see a lot of snow? What did you think about it?
- Would a little boy really be able to go around his neighborhood by himself?
- If you wanted to explore your neighborhood after a snowstorm, whom could you ask to go with you?
- Did you walk in the snow after our big snowstorm? Did you make tracks in the snow? Did you play and have fun?
- Did our big snowstorm look like Ezra Jack Keats' pictures?
- Can you tell a story about what you saw after our big snowstorm?

For 5- to 8-Year-Olds

- Can you make a tissue paper collage like Keats' bathtub picture?
- Can you make swirly clouds with cotton on blue paper like his mountain-climbing picture?
- Can you paint tracks with blue paint over white paint like his footprints picture?

ART CENTER OPTIONS

For 2- to 8-Year-Olds

- Draw a picture of a time when you explored your neighborhood.
- Draw a picture of something you saw after our big snowstorm.

For 5- to 8-Year-Olds

- Choose one of Ezra Jack Keats' techniques and make a picture of your neighborhood or of our big snowstorm.

WRITING CENTER OPTIONS

For 3- to 8-Year-Olds

- Dictate or write a sentence or story about your neighborhood.
- Dictate or write a list of surprising things you saw after our big snowstorm.
- Dictate or write a sentence or story about what your family did after our big snowstorm.

STINA

BY LENA ANDERSON

Stina visits her grandfather in his house by the sea for the summer. She watches a big storm with her grandfather who helps her feel safe and encourages her to think about the storm.

APPROPRIATE FOR:

Earthquakes
▶ **Emotional Resilience**
Epidemics and Mass Casualty Incidents
Fires and Explosions
▶ **Floods**
▶ **Hurricanes**
▶ **Shelter Experiences**
▶ **Tornadoes and Major Storms**
Volcanic Eruptions

DISCUSSION STARTERS

Use the following prompts to encourage the children to talk about their experiences, either in the context of the book or in the context of a traumatic experience.

For 5- to 8-Year-Olds

- Do you have a grandfather or other special person who makes you feel safe?

After a Traumatic Experience | Use the following prompts to invite children to talk about their experiences.
- Stina went out in the storm and felt scared. What happened next?
- What happened in our big storm (or other disaster)? Did someone help you feel safe?
- How does being safe feel?

After a Shelter Experience | Use the following prompts to invite children to talk about their shelter experiences.
- Were you able to stay in your house during our big storm (or other disaster)?
- Stina kept some treasures in a cabinet she made from a box. What kinds of treasures does she have?
- Were you able to save any of your treasures after our big storm (or other disaster)? Do you have any new treasures?

ART CENTER OPTIONS

For 3- to 8-Year-Olds

- Draw a picture of some of your old or new treasures.
- Draw a picture of someone who made you feel safe.

After a Storm or Shelter Experience
- Draw a picture of where you went in our big storm (or other disaster).

Extended Project

- Make "treasure chests" with children who lost their possessions or homes. Use sturdy cardboard boxes or other kinds of crates. Encourage the children to make or add new "treasures" to place in their treasure chests.

WRITING CENTER OPTIONS

For 3- to 8-Year-Olds

- Dictate or write a sentence or story to go with your picture.
- Write or dictate a list of your treasures.

After a Shelter Experience
- Dictate or write a letter to someone who made you feel safe in our storm (or other disaster).

STORM IN THE NIGHT

BY MARY STOLTZ AND PAT CUMMINGS (ILLUSTRATOR)

Thomas is visiting his grandfather when a big storm comes up and the lights go out. They are safe inside, and Thomas' grandfather tells stories about when he was a boy.

APPROPRIATE FOR:

Earthquakes

Emotional Resilience

Epidemics and Mass Casualty
   Incidents

Fires and Explosions

Floods

Hurricanes

Shelter Experiences

▶ **Tornadoes and Major
   Storms**

Volcanic Eruptions

DISCUSSION STARTERS

Use the following prompts to encourage the children to talk about their experiences, either in the context of the book or in the context of a traumatic experience.

For 3- to 8-Year-Olds

- Did the lights go off where you were when we had our big storm? Why?
- Did you have a flashlight when the lights went off? How did you use it?
- Did a grown-up make you feel safe when the lights went off?

For 5- to 8-Year-Olds

- Look at the illustrations by Pat Cummings:
  - ❑ She used black paper to make the house and outdoors look dark.
  - ❑ She used white chalk or paint to draw light, raindrops, and stars.

ART CENTER OPTIONS

For 3- to 8-Year-Olds

- Draw a picture of something that happened in our big storm that surprised you.
- Draw a picture of a time when you used a flashlight in the dark.

For 5- to 8-Year-Olds

- Use black paper and chalk to draw a picture of a time when the lights went off.

WRITING CENTER OPTIONS

For 3- to 8-Year-Olds

- Dictate or write a sentence or story to go with your picture.

For 5- to 8-Year-Olds

- Dictate or write a list of ways we can still get light in dark places when the electricity goes off.

TAKE TIME TO RELAX!

BY NANCY CARLSON

A big snowstorm keeps Tina and her family from doing all the things they had planned to do. They learn something about the pleasure of staying home and having time to relax.

APPROPRIATE FOR:

Earthquakes

Emotional Resilience

Epidemics and Mass Casualty
    Incidents

Fires and Explosions

Floods

Hurricanes

Shelter Experiences

▶ **Tornadoes and Major**
    Storms

Volcanic Eruptions

DISCUSSION STARTERS

Use the following prompts to encourage the children to talk about their experiences, either in the context of the book or in the context of a traumatic experience.

For 3- to 8-Year-Olds

- Does your mother or father ever work late?
- Do you ever have to eat in the car?
- Does being in a hurry ever make you feel tired or mad?
- Was our big storm like the snowstorm in Tina's story?
- When our big storm happened, did you stay at home like Tina's family, or did you go to a shelter?
- Were you able to do anything fun with your family during our big storm?

For 5- to 8-Year-Olds

- What do you think "relax" means?
- Can relaxing mean you stop feeling afraid or mad?

ART CENTER OPTIONS

For 3- to 8-Year-Olds

- Draw a picture of Tina.
- Draw a picture of you and your family during our big storm.

For 5- to 8-Year-Olds

- Draw a picture of you and your family relaxing.

WRITING CENTER OPTIONS

For 3- to 8-Year-Olds

- Dictate or write a sentence or story about where you stayed during our big storm.

For 5- to 8-Year-Olds

- Dictate or write a message to your family about how you like it when your family relaxes.

Ten Little Rubber Ducks

BY ERIC CARLE

A simple story based on an actual incident. A number of bathtub toys fall off a container ship. The little yellow ducks float off in all directions. We follow their adventures.

APPROPRIATE FOR:
Earthquakes
Emotional Resilience
Epidemics and Mass Casualty
Incidents
Fires and Explosions
► **Floods**
► **Hurricanes**
Shelter Experiences
► **Tornadoes and Major
Storms**
Volcanic Eruptions

DISCUSSION STARTERS
Use the following prompts to encourage the children to talk about their experiences, either in the context of the book or in the context of a traumatic experience.

For 3- to 8-Year-Olds
- Is this book silly? What happens in this book? What happens at the end of the story?
- Who took care of you during our hurricane (or other disaster)? How did they take care of you?
- If you told a story about our hurricane, what would happen at the end?

For 5- to 8-Year-Olds
- Look at Eric Carle's pictures:
  - The water looks like finger-painting.
  - The sun, ducks, other animals, and boat look like cut paper.
  - The white dots look like brush strokes.

ART CENTER OPTIONS
For 3- to 8-Year-Olds
- Draw a picture of what you did during our hurricane (or other disaster).

For 5- to 8-Year-Olds
- Make a picture using one of Eric Carle's techniques: finger-painting, cut-paper collage, or brush painting.

Extended Project
- Experiment with two or more of Eric Carle's art techniques.

> **After a Hurricane**
> - Combine multiple artworks, inspired by Eric Carle's techniques, and stories about our hurricane in a class exhibit.

WRITING CENTER OPTIONS
For 3- to 8-Year-Olds
- Dictate or write a sentence or story to go with your picture.

> **After a Hurricane**
> - Work with one or more children to dictate or write a counting story about our hurricane.

Extended Project
- Dictate or write a label or text panel for a classroom exhibit about our hurricane (or other disaster).

TERRIBLE STORM

BY CAROL OTIS HURST AND S.D. SCHINDLER (ILLUSTRATOR)

Two grandfathers recall the big snow of 1888. As they tell the story, each of them has his own particular memories to share.

APPROPRIATE FOR:
Earthquakes
▶ **Emotional Resilience**
Epidemics and Mass Casualty Incidents
Fires and Explosions
▶ **Floods**
▶ **Hurricanes**
▶ **Shelter Experiences**
▶ **Tornadoes and Major Storms**
Volcanic Eruptions

DISCUSSION STARTERS

Use the following prompts to encourage the children to talk about their experiences, either in the context of the book or in the context of a traumatic experience.

For 5- to 8-Year-Olds
- One of the grandfathers liked to be around a lot of people and the other one didn't.
- What is your grandfather like?
- Do you like to be around a lot of people or just a few people?
- Was the blizzard in this book kind of like our hurricane? How?
- Let's look at the drawings by S.D. Schindler. What do you see in the pictures?

After a Shelter Experience | Use the following prompts to invite children to talk about their shelter experiences.
- Was your shelter like the barn where Grandpa Otis stayed?
- Was your shelter like the big, warm house where Grandpa Clark stayed?
- What was your shelter like?
- Did the grandfathers like having to stay with strangers during the blizzard?
- Did you like staying with strangers at your shelter?

ART CENTER OPTIONS

For 5- to 8-Year-Olds
- Draw a picture of your grandfather or a favorite relative.
- Draw a picture of someone who stayed at your house one time.
- Draw a picture of a time when you stayed at someone else's house.

After a Shelter Experience
- Look at S.D. Schindler's drawings to find ideas for a picture you want to draw.
- Draw a picture of the time when you stayed in a shelter.
- Cut out magazine pictures of things you would put in a barn to make it a nice shelter.

WRITING CENTER OPTIONS

For 5- to 8-Year-Olds
- Dictate or write a sentence or story to go with your picture.

THAT SKY, THAT RAIN

BY CAROLYN OTTO AND MEGAN LLOYD (ILLUSTRATOR)

As the sky grows dark and a big storm approaches, a young girl and her grandfather move all the farm animals into the sheltering barn. Observing the gathering storm, the girl feels more mastery of the situation.

APPROPRIATE FOR:

Earthquakes
Emotional Resilience
Epidemics and Mass Casualty
   Incidents
Fires and Explosions
Floods
Hurricanes
Shelter Experiences
▶ **Tornadoes and Major Storms**
Volcanic Eruptions

DISCUSSION STARTERS

Use the following prompts to encourage the children to talk about their experiences, either in the context of the book or in the context of a traumatic experience.

For 2- to 8-Year-Olds

- Did you watch the rain in our big storm? What did you think when you saw all of the rain?
- Did the sky turn gray like the pictures in this book?
- Did any grown-ups watch the storm with you? What did you talk about while it rained?
- Did you find a place to stay out of the rain? How did it keep you dry?

For 5- to 8-Year-Olds

- Look at Megan Lloyd's pictures in this book:
  - ❏ She used watercolor paint to make the sky gray.
  - ❏ She put something red in almost every picture.

> **After a Traumatic Experience** | Use the following prompts to invite children to talk about their experiences.
> - Did you feel scared during our big storm? What did "scared" feel like?
> - Did anyone help you feel less scared? How did they help you?
> - Do you think everyone needs help when they feel scared?
> - Do you think it is okay to feel scared? Why?
> - Do grownups feel scared? How do we know?

ART CENTER OPTIONS

For 2- to 8-Year-Olds

- Draw a picture of a time during our big storm when you were scared.
- Draw a picture of something that helped you feel safe again.
- Draw a picture of a time when you were not scared.

For 5- to 8-Year-Olds

- Use black and white watercolor paint to paint a cloudy sky.
- Use some red in a picture of your house.

WRITING CENTER OPTIONS

For 3- to 8-Year-Olds

- Dictate or write a sentence or story to go with your picture.
- Dictate or write a sentence or story about where you stayed during our big storm.

For 5- to 8-Year-Olds

- Dictate or write a sentence or story about how you felt when the rain stopped to share with another child who may go through a storm.

TORNADO

BY BETSY BYARS AND
DORON BEN-AMI
(ILLUSTRATOR)

As the family waits out a tornado in the storm cellar, Pete, the farmhand, tells many stories of Tornado, the dog who arrived during another storm long ago.

APPROPRIATE FOR:

Earthquakes

Emotional Resilience

Epidemics and Mass Casualty
   Incidents

Fires and Explosions

Floods

Hurricanes

▶ **Shelter Experiences**

▶ **Tornadoes and Major
   Storms**

Volcanic Eruptions

DISCUSSION STARTERS

Use the following prompts to encourage the children to talk about their experiences, either in the context of the book or in the context of a traumatic experience.

For 5- to 8-Year-Olds

- Who tells the family stories while they are in the shelter?
- Do you know anyone who tells good stories like that?

> **After a Shelter Experience** | Use the following prompts to invite children to talk about their shelter experiences.
> - Did anyone tell stories when you were in a shelter? What stories did they tell?
> - Would you have liked to listen to stories in the shelter?

ART CENTER OPTIONS

For 5- to 8-Year-Olds

- Draw a picture of a funny dog.
- Draw a picture of a shelter in a tornado.
- Use boxes and other materials to make a model of a shelter.

WRITING CENTER OPTIONS

For 5- to 8-Year-Olds

- Dictate or write a sentence or story you would tell in a shelter.
- Dictate or write a sentence or story about your picture.
- Dictate or write a sentence or story about your model of a shelter.

> **After a Shelter Experience**
> - Dictate or write a sentence or story about the time you stayed in a shelter.

THE TORNADO WATCHES:

AN IKE AND MEM STORY

BY PATRICK JENNINGS AND ANNA ALTER (ILLUSTRATOR)

Ike and his family live in tornado country. Ike doesn't sleep well, because he worries that his family won't hear the tornado warning if it comes at night. As the story develops, his parents calmly handle everything that comes up.

Note: This chapter book is appropriate for independent readers or for reading aloud over several Circle Time periods. At the time we prepared these activities, this book was available in only 461 public libraries nationwide, less than our standard of 500. However, we include it here because it deeply explores a young boy's unspoken fears about whether his parents can protect him during a disaster.

APPROPRIATE FOR:
Emotional Resilience
Earthquakes
Epidemics and Mass Casualty
    Incidents
Fires and Explosions
Floods
Hurricanes
▶ **Shelter Experiences**
▶ **Tornadoes and Major
    Storms**
Volcanic Eruptions

DISCUSSION STARTERS

Use the following prompts to encourage the children to talk about their experiences, either in the context of the book or in the context of a traumatic experience.

For 5- to 8-Year-Olds
- What was Ike worried about?
- What did Ike's parents do?
- Did Ike help take care of someone? Who?
- What else could Ike have done when he was worried about a tornado at night?
- What did Ike find out about tornadoes?
- What did Ike find out about his parents?
- What did Ike find out about neighbors?

ART CENTER OPTIONS

For 5- to 8-Year-Olds
- Draw a picture of your family at home at night.
- Draw a picture of the room where you sleep.

After a Tornado or Severe Storm
- Draw a picture of where you and your family waited during a tornado watch.

WRITING CENTER OPTIONS

For 5- to 8-Year-Olds
- Dictate or write a list of games to keep in a storm shelter.
- Dictate or write a sentence or story about a time when you and your family waited during a tornado watch.

TOUGH TOPICS: DEATH

BY PATRICIA MURPHY

This book is part of a series that discusses situations in which children suffer and examines the emotions they may experience. It contains advice from school counselors and provides website addresses and telephone numbers for additional information or support.

APPROPRIATE FOR:
Earthquakes
▶ **Emotional Resilience**
▶ **Epidemics and Mass Casualty Incidents**
Fires and Explosions
Floods
Hurricanes
Shelter Experiences
Tornadoes and Major Storms
Volcanic Eruptions

DISCUSSION STARTERS

Use the following prompts to encourage the children to talk about their experiences, either in the context of the book or in the context of a traumatic experience.

For 5- to 8-Year-Olds
- Do you have a story about someone who died?
- Was he (or she) sick for a long time?
- Did you get to say goodbye to him (or her)? How?
- Did you go to the funeral? What was it like?
- Do you sometimes feel very sad—similar to the girl in the picture?
- What helps you feel better?

ART CENTER OPTIONS

For 5- to 8-Year-Olds
- Draw a picture of your family and friends who are alive.
- Draw a picture of a person who died.
- Draw a picture of a funeral or cemetery if you have been to one.
- Cut out photographs from magazines and glue them to paper to make a picture about someone who died.
- Make a sympathy card for the family of the person who died.

WRITING CENTER OPTIONS

For 5- to 8-Year-Olds
- Dictate or write a sentence or story about your picture.
- Dictate or write a list of things you liked about someone who has died.
- Dictate or write a message for the sympathy card.

THE VERY LONELY FIREFLY

BY ERIC CARLE

A firefly travels from place to place, looking for other fireflies. He is attracted by various kinds of light but is disappointed each time— until the final illustration, in which a group of fireflies blink in the night.

APPROPRIATE FOR:
▶ **Earthquakes**
▶ **Emotional Resilience**
  Epidemics and Mass Casualty
    Incidents
  Fires and Explosions
  Floods
  Hurricanes
  Shelter Experiences
▶ **Tornadoes and Major**
   Storms
  Volcanic Eruptions

DISCUSSION STARTERS

Use the following prompts to encourage the children to talk about their experiences, either in the context of the book or in the context of a traumatic experience.

For 2- to 8-Year-Olds
- What was the firefly looking for?
- Did you ever want to find some friends when you were lonely or it was dark?
- Did you use a flashlight when the power was off in our disaster? Did your family use a lantern?
- Did your family drive through the dark, looking for friends or a safe place to stay?
- Were you glad when you found other people or lights?

For 5- to 8-Year-Olds
- Look at the cut-paper pictures Eric Carle made by making finger-paintings and then cutting them up. Do you think you could make a picture that way?

ART CENTER OPTIONS

For 2- to 8-Year-Olds
- Draw a picture of fireflies.
- Draw a picture of a time when you and your family needed to find some lights.

WRITING CENTER OPTIONS

For 3- to 8-Year-Olds
- Dictate or write a sentence or story to go with your picture.
- Dictate or write a sentence or story about a time when you were lonely or afraid.
- Dictate or write a list of ways that your family can find light when it is dark.

VOLCANOES

BY SEYMOUR SIMON

Simon gives us comprehensive information about volcanoes around the world using understandable text and colorful illustrations.

APPROPRIATE FOR:

Earthquakes
Emotional Resilience
Epidemics and Mass Casualty
    Incidents
Fires and Explosions
Floods
Hurricanes
▶ **Shelter Experiences**
Tornadoes and Major Storms
▶ **Volcanic Eruptions**

DISCUSSION STARTERS

Use the following prompts to encourage the children to talk about their experiences, either in the context of the book or in the context of a traumatic experience.

For 5- to 8-Year-Olds

- Is this a fact book or fiction? How do you know?
- Does our volcano look like the volcanoes in these pictures?

ART CENTER OPTIONS

For 5- to 8-Year-Olds

- Use the photos in this book for ideas.
- Draw a picture of something that happened when our volcano erupted.
- Use scissors, glue, and red, yellow, and orange cellophane to make a picture of a volcano eruption.

WRITING CENTER OPTIONS

For 5- to 8-Year-Olds

- Dictate or write a sentence or story to go with your picture.
- Dictate or write a list of ways that a volcano eruption changes our landscape.

VOLCANOES AND EARTHQUAKES

BY SUSANNA VAN ROSE

Part of the DK "Eyewitness" series, this visually striking book is a non-fiction treatment of volcanoes and earthquakes, how they originate, and how they affect human life.

APPROPRIATE FOR:

▶ **Earthquakes**
  Emotional Resilience
  Epidemics and Mass Casualty
    Incidents
  Fires and Explosions
  Floods
  Hurricanes
  Shelter Experiences
  Tornadoes and Major Storms
▶ **Volcanic Eruptions**

DISCUSSION STARTERS

Use the following prompts to encourage the children to talk about their experiences, either in the context of the book or in the context of a traumatic experience.

For 5- to 8-Year-Olds
- Is this a fact book or fiction? How do you know?
- Are the pictures like our volcano eruption (or earthquake)?
- Did you and your family lose possessions in our volcano eruption (or earthquake)?
- Look at the diorama on pages 50–51 of the book: How do you think that was made?

ART CENTER OPTIONS

For 5- to 8-Year-Olds
- Draw a picture of something that happened in our volcano eruption (or earthquake).
- Refer to the pictures in the book for ideas.
- Draw a picture of something you and your family lost in our volcano eruption (or earthquake).
- Make a model of your home or another building that was damaged in our volcano eruption (or earthquake).

Extended Project
- Combine models of houses and buildings in a diorama of the community before or after the volcano eruption (or earthquake).

WRITING CENTER OPTIONS

For 5- to 8-Year-Olds
- Dictate or write a sentence or story to go with your picture.
- Dictate or write a list of possessions you and your family lost in our volcano eruption (or earthquake).

Extended Project
- Combine lists of lost possessions into a catalog of items that children and their families need help to replace.

WE HATE RAIN!

BY JAMES STEVENSON

It has been raining for two whole days, and Mary Ann and Louie are tired of it. But to Grandpa, this is just a drizzle. He has wonderful stories about when it really rained.

APPROPRIATE FOR:

Earthquakes

Emotional Resilience

Epidemics and Mass Casualty Incidents

Fires and Explosions

▶ **Floods**

Hurricanes

Shelter Experiences

▶ **Tornadoes and Major Storms**

Volcanic Eruptions

DISCUSSION STARTERS

Use the following prompts to encourage the children to talk about their experiences, either in the context of the book or in the context of a traumatic experience.

For 3- to 8-Year-Olds

- Did our big rainstorm last for weeks like the storm in this book? How long did our storm last?
- Did you play in the rain?
- Did you wonder if the rain would ever stop? What would life be like if it always rained?
- Grandpa's family ate strawberry ice cream when the rain stopped; what can we do to celebrate the end of our rainstorm?

For 5- to 8-Year-Olds

- Look at James Stevenson's cartoons:
  - ❏ Sometimes he puts a sentence below a picture.
  - ❏ Sometimes he puts what someone said in a "cloud" above the person's head.
  - ❏ What makes a cartoon different from other pictures?

ART CENTER OPTIONS

For 5- to 8-Year-Olds

- Draw a picture of what you saw in our big rainstorm.
- With a partner, draw a cartoon about our rainstorm.

WRITING CENTER OPTIONS

For 5- to 8-Year-Olds

- Dictate or write a sentence or story about your picture.
- Dictate or write words for someone in your cartoon to say.
- Dictate or write a list of things we can do while it rains.

WHEN THE BIG DOG BARKS

BY MUNZEE CURTIS AND SUSAN AVISHAI (ILLUSTRATOR)

A lot of things can be frightening to a small girl. But when her parents are nearby, she knows they will keep her safe.

Note: At the time we prepared these activities, this book was available in only 370 public libraries nationwide, less than our standard of 500. However, we include it here because it is an excellent book for helping very young children talk about frightening experiences.

APPROPRIATE FOR:
Earthquakes
Emotional Resilience
Epidemics and Mass Casualty
    Incidents
Fires and Explosions
► **Floods**
► **Hurricanes**
► **Shelter Experiences**
► **Tornadoes and Major**
    Storms
Volcanic Eruptions

DISCUSSION STARTERS

Use the following prompts to encourage the children to talk about their experiences, either in the context of the book or as a springboard to more personal discussions.

For 3- to 8-Year-Olds
- What happens when the girl climbs too high?
- What happens when the girl doesn't want to say her name?
- What happens when the girl walks past a big dog?
- Does she feel scared? How does that feel?
- Would any of those things make you feel scared? Which things?
- Did our hurricane (or other disaster) make you feel scared?
- How do people in your family keep you safe when you feel scared?

For 5- to 8-Year-Olds
- Why do you suppose Munzee Curtis wrote this book?
- Did she want children to think about the grown-ups who keep them safe?
- Look at the sentences that go with each picture.
  The sentences have a pattern:

  "When I _____, Mama (or Papa) does _____."

- Look at the drawings in the book. Susan Avishai used colored pencils and sometimes used a white pencil on top of another color.

ART CENTER OPTIONS

For 3- to 8-Year-Olds
- Experiment with colored pencils.

For 5- to 8-Year-Olds
- Draw a picture to go with your *"When I _____ ..."* sentence.

WRITING CENTER OPTIONS

For 3- to 8-Year-Olds
- Dictate or write a sentence or story about something that makes you feel scared. Dictate or write a sentence that describes how someone keeps you safe:

  "When I _____, Mama (or Papa or someone else) _____."

> **After a Hurricane**
> - Dictate or write a sentence or story about something that was scary about our hurricane (or other disaster).

WHO'S SICK TODAY?

BY LYNNE CHERRY

With rhyming language and whimsical illustrations, the author explores the familiar experience of a classmate missing because of illness. "Beavers with fevers ... stoats with sore throats...."

APPROPRIATE FOR:

Earthquakes
Emotional Resilience
▶ **Epidemics and Mass
   Casualty Incidents**
Fires and Explosions
Floods
Hurricanes
Shelter Experiences
Tornadoes and Major Storms
Volcanic Eruptions

DISCUSSION STARTERS

Use the following prompts to encourage the children to talk about their experiences, either in the context of the book or in the context of a traumatic experience.

For 2- to 8-Year-Olds
■ Do we have some sick friends in our class?
■ Is anyone in your family sick?
■ Has anyone in your family gone to a doctor?
■ Has anyone in your family gone to a hospital?

ART CENTER OPTIONS

For 3- to 8-Year-Olds
■ Draw a picture of someone who got sick.
■ Make a get-well card for someone who is sick.

For 5- to 8-Year-Olds
■ Draw a picture for a classroom exhibit about someone who got sick.

WRITING CENTER OPTIONS

For 3- to 8-Year-Olds
■ Dictate or write a sentence or story to go with your picture.
■ Dictate or write a message for the get-well card.

For 5- to 8-Year-Olds
■ Dictate or write a label or text panel for a classroom exhibit about someone who got sick.

WILLIAM AND THE GOOD OLD DAYS

BY ELOISE GREENFIELD AND JAN SPIVEY GILCHRIST (ILLUSTRATOR)

William thinks longingly about the "good old days" before Grandmother lost her sight. After a while, he begins to imagine the "good new days" when things will be different, but they still will be okay.

APPROPRIATE FOR:

Earthquakes
Emotional Resilience
▶ **Epidemics and Mass Casualty Incidents**
Fires and Explosions
Floods
Hurricanes
Shelter Experiences
Tornadoes and Major Storms
Volcanic Eruptions

DISCUSSION STARTERS

Use the following prompts to encourage the children to talk about their experiences, either in the context of the book or in the context of a traumatic experience.

For 3- to 8-Year-Olds

- How does William feel about his grandmother being sick?
- Does he feel mad? Sad? Worried?
- Do you ever feel the way William feels?

After a Family Member's Serious Illness | Use the following prompts to invite children to talk about their experiences.

- Is anyone in your family sick?
- Can you remember your family member from before he or she was sick?
- Can people who get sick get well again?

After a Family Member's Death | Use the following prompts to invite children to talk about their experiences.

- Do you think William's grandmother might die instead of get better?
- How do you think William will feel about that? What can William do to feel better?
- How did you feel when your family member died?

ART CENTER OPTIONS

For 3- to 8-Year-Olds

- Draw a picture of one of your favorite family members.
- Draw a picture of someone in your family who is sick.

After a Family Member's Death

- Draw a picture of someone in your family who died after he or she was sick.

WRITING CENTER OPTIONS

For 3- to 8-Year-Olds

- Dictate or write a sentence or story about your picture.

After a Family Member's Death

- Dictate or write a sentence or story about someone who is sick or died.

INDEX